This Book — Belongs to
Madeline Thompson.

Bible Heritage Cook Book

A Gourmet Guide to Cooking with the Bible

ROBERT L. ROBB

Triumph Publishing Co.
P.O. Box 292, Altadena, CA. 91001

© Copyright 1979 by Robert L. Robb

All rights reserved, including the right to reproduce this book, or any portions thereof, in any form, except for the inclusion of brief quotations in a review.

Library of Congress Catalog Card Number 78-059914
International Standard Book Number 0-917182-08-1

"The destiny of nations depends on how they nourish themselves." Jean Anthelme Brillat-Savarin (1755-1826)

TABLE OF CONTENTS

About the Author.. 10

Foreword.. 13

CHAPTER ONE

Garden of Eden 14

Adam's Salad... 15
A Melange of Vegetables.. 16
Dilly Cucumbers.. 17
An Eden Salad.. 18
A Euphrates Salad.. 19
A Syrian Chicken... 20
An Offering of Lamb.. 21
Potatoes LaLanne... 21
Apple Pie.. 22
Jerusalem Falafel.. 23
Higos Frescos Al Licor... 24

CHAPTER TWO

The Time Between 25

Introduction... 25
Middle East Herbed Dove.. 26
Garlic Olives.. 27
Savory Shortribs... 28
A Negev Steak.. 29
A Festive Roast Goose.. 30
Plum Sauce... 31
A Tangerine Game Hen... 31
Tangerine Sauce.. 32
A Jordan Chicken... 33
Lemon Barbecued Chicken.. 34
Flowered Potatoes.. 34
Braised Leeks Gourmet.. 36
A Medley of Gourds... 37

4

Biblical Lentils.. 38
Wined Halibut Steaks.. 38
A Nile Duck.. 39
Egyptian Green Beans....................................... 41

CHAPTER THREE

On the Exodus Trail 42

Introduction... 42
Exodus Quail, First Miracle on the Trail............ 43
Manna, The Second Miracle on the Trail.......... 45
Matzo Bread... 46
A Wagon Train Bread....................................... 47
Braised Pheasant.. 48
Peanut Chicken a la Carter............................... 49
Chicken Citrus.. 50
Barbecued Short Ribs....................................... 52
Dilled Veal Shoulder Steaks.............................. 53
Abraham's Veal Cutlets.................................... 54
Lamb Saffron Stew 55
Grill Roasted Onions... 56
Jerusalem White Beans.................................... 56
Cheesed White Beans....................................... 57
Persian Meatballs 58
Tomato Dip (for Iraq Meatballs)....................... 59
Potato Dough for Iraqui Meatballs 60
Kibbeh.. 60
Pharaoh's Bread... 61
Peaches a la Sinhue.. 62
Sardine Sandwiches.. 63
A Sabra Dessert.. 64

CHAPTER FOUR

In the Wilderness 66

Introduction... 66

Marinated Lamb Steaks.................................... 67
Jordan Almond Chicken.................................. 68
A Fruited Cornish Game Hen............................ 69
Josephus Meat Balls..................................... 70
A Traveler's Stew.. 71
Hash from Kadesh.. 72
Braised Short Ribs....................................... 73
A Wilderness Barbecue................................... 75
An Almond Orange Bread................................ 76
A Heavenly Trout.. 77
Fruit of the Desert....................................... 77
Wine Introduction....................................... 79
Wine Herbed Veal.. 80
Wined Chicken Livers.................................... 80
Spicy Figs.. 81
(A Joyous White Sauce.)................................. (82)
A Savory Dove... 83
A Desert Nut Cake....................................... 84

CHAPTER FIVE

Canaan 86

Spice Introduction....................................... 86
An Appetizer from Sheba................................ 87
Arabic Tangerine.. 88
Solomon's Saffron Chicken 89
King Solomon's Roast 91
Tangerine Glazed Cornish Game Hens 92
Saucy Tangerine Glaze 92
Duro Wat 92
Niter Kebbeh 93
Berbere 94
Doro Wat Chicken 95
A Royal Goose 96
The Plum Sauce 97
Joyous Chicken.. 98
Pate of Duck.. 100

A Tarshish Turkey	101
Turkey Turkish Thighs	103
Wine Braised Lamb	104
Dolmas	105
Roast Saddle of Lamb	106
A Skewered Veal Dish from Moab	107
Orange Stuffed Loin of Lamb	108
A Salad from Marib, the Capitol of Sheba	109
Injera	110
Jaa Whole Wheat Bread	111
King's Bread	112
A Lebanese Injurada	113
A Red Sea Tahineh	114
A Mediterranean Paella	115
A Palestine Gourmet Dinner	116
Lois' Biblical Meat Loaf	117
A Wilderness Braised Beef	118
Israel Cholent	119
Tented Pot Roast	120
African Eggplant Stew	121
A Faithful Potatoe Salad	122
Festive Raisins	123
A Carrot Cake	124
An Almond Delight	124
An Almond Honey	125

CHAPTER SIX

The Time of Christ — 126

A Golden Scimitar Appetizer	127
A Little Appetizer	128
A Hot Onion Appetizer	129
Cheese Introduction	129
Cheese Definitions	130
A Cheese Strata	133
A Wined Cheddar Cheese	134
A Mount Olivet Salad	135
An Arabian Salad	136
Arabian Skewered Lamb	137
A Turkey Salmis	138

Israeli Orange Chicken... 139
Elijah's Potage 140
Matzo Marrow Balls 140
Chicken of the Earth.. 141
Southern Fried Chicken... 142
Chicken Salmis... 144
Fish Introduction... 145
Fish Chowder for the Multitude................................... 145
A Tiberian Carp.. 147
A Bonito from Tyre... 147
A Stuffed Baked Bass... 149
A Festival Fish 150
Sea Bass A La Canaan 151
Swedish Glassblowers Herring 151
Wined Halibut Steaks 152
A Centurian's Lamb.. 153
A Roast of Galilee.. 155
Beef from the Fertile Crescent..................................... 156
An Herder's Steak.. 157
A Range Rider's Stew... 158
Orange Fig Bread... 159
Challah 160
Angelic Raisin Bread.. 162
A Lentil Stuffed Bread.. 162
Dessert Introduction.. 163
Orange Pound Cake.. 164
A Memphis Dessert... 165
A Refreshing Water Ice... 166

CHAPTER SEVEN

Three Gourmet Dinners

Dinner No. 1:
   Introduction 168
   Caviar 169
   Blini.. 170

Consume Julienne
   (the Bullion) 171
   (the Consumme) 172
Trout Tobyshka 173
Roast Baron of Lamb 175
Endive Salade 176

Dinner No. 2:
   Braised Celery 177
   Vichysoisse 178
   A Filet of Sole 179
   White Wine Sauce 180
   Yorkshire Pudding 181
   A Rare English Roast Beef 182
   Caesar Salad 183
   Ice Cream Roll 184

Dinner No. 3:
   A Ginger Cheese 186
   Mushrooms Angelic 186
   An Oasis Stuffed Egg 187
   A Royal Hors D'Oeuvre 188
   Lebanese Dip 189
   Sherried Consumme 189
   Fillets of Sole In White Wine 190
   White Wine Sauce 191
   Kalu Filet Oscar 193
   Chilled Dessert Melon Cups 194
   Glazed Tangerine Ambrosia 194

ABOUT THE AUTHOR

Bob Robb was born Robert Lincoln Robb in Pueblo, Colorado. He grew up in San Jose, California and attended both Fresno and San Jose State Colleges. He began his professional career as an actor/announcer in radio while still in school and soon was directing plays at the San Jose Community Playhouse.

When World War II began, Robb's intense interest in aviation drew him to enlist in the Air Force, and after completing basic training, he became the Chief Clerk of the Intelligence Division at Moffet Field and later, at Santa Ana AFTB. After graduating from Officer's Candidate School in 1942, he served with the 96th Bomb Group in England for two years. In 1944, he was called to Sweden to supervise and care for the 1800 U.S. airmen that were interned there and became the Executive Officer of the Military and Military Air Attaches Office, with full diplomatic rank. He traveled extensively throughout Europe during this time. Returning to the U.S. in 1947, he continued to be active in the Reserves, rising to the rank of Major and the presidency of the Reserve Officers Association.

Robb first joined ABC-Radio in 1947 as Director of Continuity Acceptance and began directing television in 1950. From 1953 to 1955, he also served as president of the Radio and Television Directors Guild. During the thirteen years Robb was with ABC, he directed a wide variety of shows; from "Space Patrol" to cooking shows, where he directed and learned from such luminaries in that field as Grace Lawson, James Beard, Helen Evans Brown, Elena of San Francisco and many, many others.

He also became one of the industry's finest commercial directors, handling for many years, the Dodge, Plymouth and Chrysler commercials on shows such as Lawrence Welk, Steve Allen, Garry Moore, Chrysler Theatre and Playhouse 90. Among the hundreds of food commercials he has directed are the giants of the industry: Standard Brands, General Foods, Hunt's and Kraft Foods.

Robb directed the nation's first television tape from Hawaii, utilizing video tape machines that he borrowed from the Air Force for the occasion. He left ABC, to direct all the television for the first U.S. political campaign that utilized fully, this media that has since become so vital to the electoral process: the Brown vs. Nixon campaign for the governorship of California. Brown won.

In 1962, he joined KTLA—Channel 5, Golden West Broadcasters in Los Angeles, and has continued to do the incredible variety of programs that mark his career; commercials, game shows, telethons, documentaries, specials, fashion shows, series such as the world famous "Divorce Court," and of course, cooking shows.

Over the years, as his wide circle of friends and experiences grew, Robb met many people who shared his interests and especially his interest in food. Among his gourmet friends have been found Ture Wretman, who owns the Opera Kjellaren Restaurant in Stockholm, Major General Count Folke Bernadotte, who was the first United Nations mediator to Palestine, Bengt Nordenskiold, chief of the Swedish Air Force, General George Patton, General James Doolittle, President Herbert Hoover, Knut Veeijk, president of the Swedish Steamship Lines, and Jimmy Stewart, Zsa Zsa Gabor, Vincent Price, Elroy "Crazy-legs" Hirsch, Elton Rule, president of ABC, Tom Sarnoff, president of NBC, Adolph Zukor, Chet Huntley, Corris Guy, Jack La Lanne, Chef Mike Roy and hundreds of other fascinating people.

Robb has amassed an enormous collection of cookbooks and recipes from around the world, not including his own recipes which fill eight loose leaf binders to overflowing. For years a genial and generous host to his friends, he was finally prevailed upon by Lawry's Foods (the restaurant chain and makers of their famous Seasoned Salt, spices and dressings) to give cooking classes at their beautiful "California Center" in Los Angeles. The classes are among the most successful that Lawry's has had, and the always constant pressure from his friends, to write his own cookbook, continued. He certainly had the material and the experience, but he still felt he needed a very special reason to write a very special book.

Born into a pioneering family, Robb was raised by loving and deeply religious parents. His father, a butcher and his mother an excellent cook, love of God and an interest in food and it's preparation combined very early in his life. His subsequent professional career carried him to many parts of the world and gave him an extraordinary opportunity to explore the food of many countries, and everywhere, he wondered at the incredible bounty that God has provided for Man. That wonder became the inspiration for this book.

The Bible Heritage Cook Book: A Gourmet Guide to Cooking with the Bible is both a celebration of and a thanks-giving for, that bounty. Filled with interesting, healthful recipes for natural foods, spiced with Biblical history, and quotations from the Bible, it is Robb's way to say "Thank you, Lord, from all of us!"

FOREWORD

The Bible. Timeless book of the ages.

A living chronicle about people and events, hopes and fears, courage and belief.

The great story of the creation.

The story, too of over one million men, women, and children who wandered in the wilderness for 40 years and reached the "Promised Land," only to find that they constantly had to defend themselves in order to survive.

And survive they did!

The "Promised Land" became the focal point of GOD's law and love through the people's courage. And it was the place where the Christian religion was born.

A study of the Bible reveals the great bounty the Lord gave all mankind. Hundreds and thousands of varieties of plants, species of fish, fowls, animals, herbs and spices.

And the fascinating narrations of the people of Biblical times, their customs and festivals, all evidence their appreciation of God's gifts of food.

The stories of the First and Second miracles during the Exodus on the Plains of the Wilderness of Sin; the story of King Solomon and the Queen of Sheba, and the miracle of the loaves and fishes by Jesus all became part of the wonderful story of God and his people.

There are more than a thousand mentions of food in the Bible. As then, all of today's people enjoy them, and it is my hope that this book will help you enjoy them even more. It is a labor of love and of reverence. I pray that you and yours will enjoy many memorable meals from this book, and through it gain a deeper appreciation of the Creation and the Lord's gifts.

Most sincerely,

Bob Robb

Chapter One

The Garden of Eden

The Bible relates that on the 3rd, 5th, and 6th days of the creation, the Lord God made to grow all the cattle and creeping things, beasts, fowls of the air, fish of the sea, herbs, grass, and every fruit tree yielding seed.

And over it all he gave dominion to man.

"And God said, let us make man in our image, after our likeness; and let them have dominion over the fish of the sea, and over the fowl of the air, and over the cattle, and over all the earth, and over every creeping thing that creepeth upon the earth" (Genesis 1: 26).

And then following his seventh day of rest, the Lord God planted a garden.

"And the Lord God planted a garden, Eastward in Eden, and there he put the man he had formed.

"And out of the ground, the Lord God made to grow every tree that is pleasant to the sight and good for food" (Genesis 2: 8-9).

Visualize this vast garden if you will. Fields of grains, trees of every kind bearing fruit and nuts, sprouting vines carry gourds, melons, promegranates, and grapes. Vegetables of every sort spring from the ground. Bountiful fish in the rivers, seas, and lakes. Birds flying overhead, and in the distance, herds of cattle and sheep.

And yet, according to the scripture, Adam threw it all over for just one bite of the forbidden fruit!

Even so the Lord was good to Adam and Eve, for he obviously let him take with him, when he was expelled, the seeds and the cuttings and whatever else he needed to survive. And we today, are the fortunate inheritors of this bounty, for all that we eat and drink is in part a descendant of those biblical gifts.

However, let us return to Adam while he was still the master of the Garden of Eden, and see how well he fared in the first land of plenty.

He must have had at hand fruits of all kinds, nuts, spices, vegetables, grains, olives, and, of course, beef and lamb. And if you were in the midst of all this plenty, and in a creative cooking mood, you might have made:

ADAM'S SALAD

2 large peeled cucumbers
1/2 unpeeled cucumber
1/3rd cup water
1 envelope unflavored gelatin
1 pint whipped sour cream
1/4th cup lemon juice
1 tsp lemon extract
2 tbs honey
1 tsp grated lemon peel
2 tbs minced mint leaves
1/2 cup whole mint leaves
1/2 tsp salt
1/4th tsp fresh ground black pepper

Thinly slice the 2 large cucumbers, sprinkle the slices with salt and let them stand in a bowl for about 30 minutes.

During this time dissolve the gelatin in the water, in a double boiler over hot water, and then combine it with all the remaining ingredients.

Now, in a round 6 cup mold, put the cucumber slices (which have been rinsed and drained), using about 1/3rd of them in a bottom layer. Then pour over half the cream mixture. Then he would arrange the remaining cucumber slices on top, and cover with the rest of the sour cream mixture. Cover and let chill in the refrigerator for about 6 hours.

Now turn the mold out onto a chilled plate, and take the 1/2 cucumber you have saved; score it and slice it thinly. Lay these slices overlapping on top and surround the mold with sprigs of whole mint and parsley.

This will serve 6 or 8 on a lovely summer's day in your personal "Garden of Eden"!

"And God said, Let the earth bring forth grass, the herb yielding seed, and the fruit tree yielding fruit after his kind, whose seed is in itself, upon the earth, and it was so" (Genesis 1: 11).

The eternal God blessed us with so many of the fruits of the land and sea that it is sometimes difficult to decide how to prepare them. A relatively simple way to make use of several vegetables is one that calls on your ingenuity. This way of doing it I call:

A MELANGE OF VEGETABLES

1/2 cup olive oil
1 cup thinly sliced onions
1 clove garlic, chopped
2 zuchini, thickly sliced
1 medium eggplant, peeled and sliced
1/2 cup flour
2 green peppers, cut in strips
2 tomatoes, cut in wedges
a tsp salt
1/4th tsp oregano
1/4th tsp rosemany
1/8th tsp pepper

Please use a flameproof ceramic dish for this, as it is prepared atop the stove. Firstly, heat the olive oil and then add the garlic and onions and cook very gently until they are tender, but not browned.

Dip the squash and the eggplant in the flour and coat lightly. Then combine with the green pepper strips and place in the dish along with the garlic-onion mixture.

Cover and simmer for about 30 minutes.

Then add the tomatoes, oregano, rosemary and pepper, and salt. Cover again and simmer for about 15 minutes.

This will make 8 to 10 servings as a side dish.

One version of the Bible describes cucumbers as heavy and hard to digest. In Hebrew they are *Kishuim*. Originally they were grown only in the fertile land which is overflowed by the Nile, but they were also esteemed to be the coolest and most pleasant fruit in the East.

> *"And the daughter of Zion is left as a cottage in a vineyard, as a lodge in a garden of cucumbers, as a besieged city"* (Isaiah 1: 8).

However they are regarded, when they are combined with Dill which was also common to the lands of the Mediterranean, they make a most palatable dish, which might be termed . . .

"DILLY" CUCUMBERS

3 large firm shiny cucumbers
1 tbs salt
1/2 cup cider vinegar
1/4th cup tarragon vinegar
2 tbs sugar
1/8th tsp white pepper
1 tsp dill seeds
1 tbs finely minced parsley

Wash the cucumbers, peel them, and then slice them rather thickly (about 1/8th inch). Sprinkle them with the salt, press them down with a weighted plate and let them stand for 30 minutes.

Rinse them and drain them thoroughly. Combine them with the sugar, pepper, and the dill seeds, along with the vinegar and parsley.

Put the salad in the refrigerator for a time to chill, and serve with some delectable lamb, and some gently browned new potatoes.

> *"And God said, behold I have given you every herb bearing seed, which is upon the face of all the Earth, and every tree in which is the fruit of a tree bearing seed: to you it shall be for meat"* (Genesis 1: 29).

Although the lettuce familiar to Adam and Eve was not quite like the highly cultivated lettuce we know today (it grew on tall stalks with the loose leaves), it was just as tasty and often used to augment a meal.

This recipe is for a simple salad, which I have found most useful and easy to prepare. I call it . . .

AN EDEN SALAD

1 small head of Romaine lettuce
2 medium tomatoes, quartered
4 green onions, chopped with the green tops included
some garlic croutons
1/2 cup pitted black olvies
1/2 cup pitted green olives

THE DRESSING:
1 clove of garlic, crushed
1/2 tsp salt
1/2 tsp dry mustard
3 tbs red wine vinegar
6 to 8 tbs olive oil

Prepare this some time before dinner and let it chill. You'll find it goes well with almost any kind of meat.

First, wash the lettuce, and then tear it into bite-sized pieces. Add the tomatoes and the chopped green onion.

Make the dressing by crushing the garlic clove into the salt, then add the mustard and mix well. Add the wine vinegar and mix again. Finally add the olive oil and mix again.

One easy way to do the mixing is to put the combination of salt, garlic, and mustard into a jar, and add the vinegar and olive oil and cover with a tight fitting lid and shake well.

Pour this dressing over the salad greens, and just before serving top with the garlic croutons.

Serve this with a fine steak or some broiled chops.

> "And a river went out of Eden to water the garden, and from thence it was parted, and became into four heads. The name of the first is Pison: That is it that compasseth the whole land of Havilah, where there is gold; And the gold of that land is good: there is Bdellium and the onyx stone.
>
> "And the name of the second river is Gihon: The same is it that compasseth the whole land of Ethiopia.
>
> "And the name of the third river is Hiddekel: that is it which goeth toward the east of Assyria. And the fourth river is Euphrates" (Genesis 2: 10-13).

Wherever these great rivers ran, they formed great deltas, which were used by the people to grow their crops. Even now the delta of the Euphrates is used to grow fruits and vegetables of all kinds. One of the more important vegetables cultivated is the lovely purple eggplant. Here is one way to enjoy its succulance:

A EUPHRATES SALAD

1 large eggplant, purple and firm
1/4th cup Miracle Whip
2 hard boiled eggs, chopped
1/2 cup finely chopped sweet pickles
1/4th cup EACH finely chopped mint and green onion
1/2 tsp garlic powder
3 tbs olive oil
2 tbs lemon juice
Salt & pepper
Lemon wedges
Cherry tomatoes
Thin sliced sweet red onions
Pumpernickel or dark rye bread

On the banks of the Euphrates, you would:
Cook the eggplant in a very hot oven, until it is well charred on the outside and soft inside. Let it cool, and peel it and coarsely chop the inner meat.
Put this in a bowl and mix in the Miracle Whip, pickles, eggs, mint and onions, olive oil, lemon juice and the salt and pepper to taste.
Transfer to a 4 to 6 cup mold and chill thoroughly.
When ready, unmold onto a chilled platter and garnish with the onion slices, lemon wedges, and the cherry tomatoes. A few fresh sprigs of mint or watercress will give it added color.
Serve with dark rye or pumpernickel bread.

> *"And out of the ground, the Lord GOD formed every beast of the field, and every fowl of the air, and brought them to Adam to see what he would call them" (Genesis 2:19).*

Chickens of some kind and their eggs must have been well known to our ancestors.
This is an interesting Mediterranean method of preparing chicken in an earthenware dish, and it will make the basis of a fine supper.

A SYRIAN CHICKEN

4 tbs butter
A 4 to 5 lb roasting chicken
1 large onion, finely chopped
1/4th cup celery, finely chopped
2 tbs chopped parsley
1-1/2 cups tomato juice
1 chicken bouillon cube
1/2 tsp salt
1/4th tsp pepper
1/2 tsp thyme
6 black olives, pitted and sliced
6 green olives, pitted and sliced
1 pimento, sliced in strips

GO PICK YOUR OLIVES AND THEN:
Melt the butter in a skillet and lightly brown the chicken on all sides. Remove the chicken and reserve and then gently saute' the onion, celery, and parsley in the remaining butter for 3 to 5 minutes until the onion is soft, but not browned. Add the tomato juice and the bullion cube and stir until the cube is melted and the mixture is hot.

Truss the chicken and place in a deep earthenware pot.

Pour over the tomato sauce, from the skillet, and season the chicken with salt, pepper and thyme.

Cover and roast in a pre-heated 400-F oven for two hours until the chicken is juicy tender.

Remove the chicken from the pot, strain the juices and add the olives. Put the sauce in another saucepan and simmer for several minutes. Return the chicken to the earthenware pot and pour the sauce over before serving.

"And Abel, he also brought of the firstlings of his flock and of the fat thereof. And the Lord had respect unto Abel and to his offering" (Genesis 4: 4).

From the very beginning Lamb was used in the ritual services devoted to the Lord. But it was also regarded as a fine food, and this Middle East method of preparation will certainly be proof of the pudding!

AN OFFERING OF LAMB

1/2 cup dried white, kidney beans
2-1/2 lbs boneless lamb shoulder meat
2 tbs olive oil
1/2 cup chopped onion
2 (8 oz) cans tomato sauce
1 tbs lemon juice
1 tsp salt
1/2 tsp EACH oregano, thyme, and tumeric
1/4th tsp EACH pepper and ground cinnamon
1 Bay leaf

TO OFFER THIS TO YOUR LOVED ONES, YOU SHOULD...
Soak the beans in cold water overnight and then drain them.

Cook them in boiling salted water for 15 minutes and then drain them again. Brown the lamb pieces in the hot olive oil and add the onion and cook until it is tender.

In a large pot, put in the beans, lamb, and add the onions, tomato sauce, 1/4th cup water, lemon juice, salt, oregano, thyme, tumeric, pepper, cinammon and bay leaf. Cover and simmer for 1-1/2 hours until meat and beans are tender. Skim off any excess fat before serving.

"To everything there is a season, and a time to every purpose under the heaven" (Ecclesiastes 3: 1).

I believe a fine friend of mine, Jack Lalanne, would subscribe to that Biblical concept most heartily, as Jack is a man who believes in using the right thing at the right time. And by doing so he has kept himself in prime physical condition all his life.

Potatoes are not specifically mentioned in the Bible, but they certainly are part of "herbs and things" that God caused the earth to produce, and their various varieties are seasonal. This recipe, created by Jack Lalanne, has long been a favorite of mine, and I think you will like it as well.

POTATOES LALANNE

4 White Rose potatoes
2 tbs olive oil
Salt and Pepper

Jack is a proponent of good health food, and as such, prepares and preaches the kinds of foods that must have been used by the folk of the Bible. Simple fare, but full of nutrition, capable of sustaining one for long periods of time.

What Jack does is thoroughly scrub the potatoes, and then slice them in fairly thick slices, without peeling them. Jack has a saying that with all of the parings that go into our sinks, we must have the healthiest garbage disposals in the world!

Next he arranges the slices of potato on a cookie sheet in an even layer; sprinkles them with salt and the olive oil, and puts them under the broiler until nicely browned.

Then he turns them over, using a bit more salt and olive oil and browns the other side.

These can be served with eggs, roast beef, lamb chops, or whatever.

Try them, you'll be in for a taste treat!

Aside from the tomato, which was once regarded as poison, the apple has probably been the most maligned fruit of the earth.

But, really, was it an apple that Adam was offered by a most lovely lady? Mythology says it was, but we really don't know what Eve offered to Adam.

Actually, as the centuries rolled by, apples became an important part of religion as well as diet. One of Hercules' tasks was to obtain the golden apples of the Heresperides. And where would we all be without the Law of Gravity, which was supposedly discovered by Newton, when an apple fell and hit him on the head!

As far as America is concerned, apples were planted far and wide by our ancestors, largely because of their many uses as food, and for their nutritive value. Remember Johnny Appleseed?

However, had Adam known of it, it is quite possible he would have asked Eve to bake him an:

APPLE PIE *Try This*

6 cups cooking apples: McIntosh, York Imperial, Jonathans, or Northern Spy
3/4ths to 1 cup sugar
1 teaspoon ground cinamon
3 tablespoons butter
Pastry for a 2-crust, 9-inch pie, unbaked

THE VERSES

Line a 9-inch pie pan with pastry. Actually the frozen pie pastry that you can buy in most supermarkets works very well for this. In a bowl, mix the cinnamon and the sugar. Add the apples, which have been peeled, cored, and sliced and mix well. When you prepare the apples, place them in a large bowl of cold water so they will not turn brown. You can also add a little lemon juice if you like to keep them nice and white.

Heap the apple-spice mixture in the crust lined pan, and dot with butter. Place the top crust over and cut slits with a sharp knife so the steam can escape. Seal the edges by moisturing with a bit of water all around. Now flute the edges with a fork to make it as attractive as possible.

Bake in a pre-heated hot over (425-F) for about 50 minutes, until the apples are done and the top is light brown and crisp. If the edges seem to be getting too brown, cover them with some strips of foil.

Serve this beautiful gift either hot or cold, with lots of thick cream, or ice cream, or cheese. I guarantee you will give thanks with every savory mouthful.

> *"For a friend of mine in his journey is come to me, and I have nothing to set before him"* (Luke 11: 6).

One thing that might have been set before his friend is an appetizer that quite probably originated in Egypt and was carried across the Red Sea as a recipe in the minds of the Israelites is Falafel. It is a popular dish throughout all of the Middle East, and is one that can be eaten at almost any time of the day. Falafel is made from Pea Beans, which are very popular in the Southwestern United States where they are called Garbanzos.

JERUSALEM FALAFEL *Try this*

1/2 lb chick peas
Salt, white pepper
2 eggs, slightly beaten
3 tbs melted shortening
2 tbs bread crumbs
1/2 tsp onion powder
1/2 tsp cumin
1 small hot red chili pepper
2 tbs lemon juice
1 tbs honey

Salad Oil
Peta Bread pieces

THE WAY TO PREPARE:

Soak the chick peas overnite in cold water. Drain; place in a saucepan and cover again with water. Add 1 tbs salt and bring to a boil. Reduce the flame and simmer for 2 hours or until the beans are very tender.

Add water when necessary to keep the peas covered during the cooking. Let cool and drain.

Put through a meat grinder using the fine blade, or mash in a blender. Add 1/2 tsp salt, 1/4th tsp white pepper, the eggs, melted shortening, bread crumbs, chili powder, cumin, onion powder, lemon juice and the honey. Blend thoroughly and chill.

Form into balls about 1/2-inch in diameter. In a skillet, preheat the oil and then fry the balls until they are brown. Sprinkle with salt and serve hot. Falafel may also be inserted into warm Peta Bread and served with a cold salad as a luncheon piece.

"And the Trees said to the Fig Tree, Come thou and reign over us." (Judges 9:10)

HIGOS FRESCOS AL LICOR:
(Fresh Figs with Liqueur)

Fresh figs
Cinnamon
Confectioner's sugar
Malaga wine
Fundador Brandy
Cinnamon sticks

Put washed fresh figs in a deep serving dish. Cover to about 1/3rd their depth with cinnamon and confectioner's sugar dissolved in Malaga wine and Brandy, (or Grand Marnier, Chartreuse, or Cointreau). Using the following proportions:

1 8-oz. glass wine to 1 shot glass brandy, 1 tsp cinnamon, and 2 to 4 tsps sugar. Sprinkle fig tops with more confectioner's sugar and cinnamon, and serve fruit with more liqueur. Garnish with cinnamon sticks.

Chapter Two

The Time Between

Not too much is known about the times after Adam and Eve were expelled from the Garden and when the Lord caused the flood. Development of the land outside Eden started with Adam's farming, and, of course, there was the birth of Abel and then Cain. Abel also became a good farmer and used herds of sheep. More and more people were born, which naturally required more and more food.

Trees were planted, vegetables grown, grains were cultivated, and animals raised and slaughtered.

Unfortunately, mankind also cultivated a great deal of evil, to the point where the Lord decided to cleanse the earth and start all over with Noah and the contents of the Ark. And so there were forty days and nights of rain.

When the waters finally receded and returned to the rivers and the seas, the land was free again to grow it's bounty and give mankind a fresh start on life.

At the Lord's instruction, Noah had all the necessary seeds, and other growing things, as well as the animals needed to refurnish the earth.

> *"And take thou unto thee of all food that is eaten, and thou shalt gather it to thee; and it shall be food for thee, and for them" (Genesis 6:21).*

Little by little the world started to come to life and the descendents of Noah and the animals of the Ark began to populate the earth.

> *"And the dove came into him in the evening; and lo, in her mouth was an olive leaf pluckt off: so Noah knew that the waters were abated from off the earth" (Genesis 8:11).*

The dove with an olive branch held firmly in it's beak has been a symbol of peace for generations. It can be supposed that Noah and his family took this dove to indicate that GOD was once again at peace with the earth, and it's people, following the 40 days and 40 nights of the great flood.

Doves are also very fine eating, and if you happen to have some fresh grape leaves handy, you might try this Middle Eastern way of preparing them.

MIDDLE EAST HERBED DOVES

6 doves, plucked and cleaned
6 tbs soft butter
½ cup chopped fresh rosemary or ¼th cup dried
¼ cup dry white wine
6 large or 11 medium sized grape leaves
Aluminum foil

Very lightly salt and pepper the birds, inside and out. Place some of the rosemary in the cavity of each bird. Make an herbed butter sauce by melting the butter and then adding the remaining rosemary and the wine. Simmer it gently for just a moment and then set aside.

Place a well washed and drained grape leaf on a piece of foil large enough to completely encompass the bird.

Place each bird on a grape leaf, and pour over it some of the herbed butter sauce. Tightly wrap the foil around the grapeleaf and the bird, and seal the ends tightly.

Place them in a shallow pan and roast them in a 350-F oven for about 1½ hours or until they are tender. Serve them on a "Trencher" made by cutting french rolls in half and scooping out enough of the center to make a cup for the bird. Butter and toast them lightly, and then carefully unwrap the birds and place each one, (removing the grape leaf) on a bread cup. Pour any of the sauce and juices that remain in the foil over the birds and garnish them with parsley or watercress.

Serve with a crisp tossed green salad and a fine, well chilled, Vin Rose wine!

"His branches shall spread, and his beauty shall be as the olive tree" (Hosea 14:6).

Just as necessary to the livelihood of the early world as were their sheep and fish and cattle, were olives.

Olive trees provided wood for construction, as well as fuel; oil for cooking, and their fruit for good nutritive eating, both dried and preserved.

The Mount of Olives, which figured prominently in Christ's life as well as that of his disciples is mentioned many times in the Bible.

> *"And when they had sung a hymn, they went out into the Mount of Olives" (Matthew 26:30).*

The origin of the olive has been attributed to Asia, and it is estimated that olive trees were cultivated in the Mediterranean area since about 3,000 years before Christ.

Early denizens of this area could not have lived without them, as they provided the essential fat in their diet. In fact they were once considered sacred, and the cutting down of an olive tree was considered a serious crime.

Perhaps one way you can celebrate an evening of peace and pleasurable dining is to serve:

GARLIC OLIVES
(or The Lion and the Lamb)

1 medium sized jar, pitted green olives
2 cloves garlic, peeled and sliced
4 dried red chili peppers
1½ tbs red wine vinegar
1 tsp dried Dill weed

Drain the olives, reserving the liquid in a small saucepan, and put the olives aside.

Add the garlic and chili peppers to the olive liquid in the pan. Bring to a boil, lower the heat and simmer gently for 5 minutes. Now add the vinegar and the dillweed. Pour over the olives and let them cool.

Pack into a nice clean jar; cover, and chill.

> *"And I will send grass in thy fields for the cattle, that Thou mayest eat and be full" (Deuteronomy 11:15).*

To eat and be full is the dream of just about everyone on earth.

The arduous tasks required of the people of early times, must have made them very hungry by nightfall, and it was then the task of the housewife to have a hearty meal prepared. One that would satisfy her hungry family.

A beef, taken from their herd, often served this need, as it was nutritious, filled with protein, and imparted energy. We eat it today for the same reasons, and one way you might emulate the housewife of yore, is by cooking:

SAVORY SHORTRIBS

Flour
Salt & Pepper
4 lbs shortribs cut into pieces
3 tbs olive oil
1 large onion, sliced
1 clove garlic, minced
2 cups beef stock
1 tbs sugar
2 tbs mustard
2 tbs red wine vinegar
1/8th tsp cinnamon
1/4th tsp grated fresh ginger
10 dried prunes
10 dried apricots
noodles
1/4 cup milk

Mix together the flour, salt and pepper. Smear the mustard over the ribs and then cover them with the flour mixture. Brown the ribs in the olive oil, then remove and reserve. Saute the onions in the liquid in which you have browned the ribs, just until they start to turn color.

Return the meat to the Dutch oven, add the beef stock, sugar, vinegar, cinnamon, and ginger. Bring to a boil, cover, and simmer for 1½ to 2 hours.

Remove the ribs to a serving platter and keep warm. Skim off as much fat as possible from the liquid in the pot, and add 1/4th cup of the seasoned flour used in the beginning to coat the ribs. Stir in 1/4th cup milk, and cook and stir until the gravey thickens. Now add the prunes and apricots, which have previously softened in hot water, and salt the gravy to taste. Serve with noodles, smothered with the fruits and gravy.

"And Abraham was very rich in cattle, in silver, and in gold"
(Genesis 13:2).

What we do today as a summer outdoor exercise was probably the major method of cooking for the seekers of the Promised Land.

Barbecuing can provide a superb gourmet meal, and the preparation of it can be a fine art, providing either a fine lunch or a great dinner.

More than any other meat, Beef lends itself to grilling, roasting, and spit cooking. It can be barbecued a hundred different ways, using marinades, sauces, relishes, and whatever. And almost every cut of beef is usable.

I'm quite certain the Israel herders of cattle in Egypt had a beef cut, approximating what we would term today, a steak. Cooked over glowing coals it can turn out to be a rare and tasty treat!

Let's pretend it is night in the desert. The firmament is clear, and the stars are sparkling. And set before you, after your hard day's labours, is a slightly charred steak, thick, hot and juicy inside, that has been marinated, and then roasted just the proper distance from the fire to give it that special flavor and doneness.

Here's how a Desert Herder might have cooked,

"A NEGEV STEAK"

2 to 4 rib steaks
2 bunches green onions
1½ cups Chablis wine
½ cup wine vinegar
Salt and freshly ground black pepper
1 tsp seasoned salt
2 to 4 sprigs fresh parsley

Place the steaks in a shallow dish and after thoroughly mixing the chopped green onions, wine, vinegar, seasoned salt, and the salt and pepper, pour the mixture over the steaks and let them soak up the flavors for 3 or 4 hours.

Grill the steaks to a turn that pleases your taste, and just before serving them, top them with the parsley which has been cooked in some melted butter.

While you are at it, saute some french fry sized potatoes and prepare some fresh green peas to go along with the steaks.

> *"Behold the fowls of the air: for they sow not, neither do they reap, nor gather into barns; yet your heavenly father feedeth them" (Matthew 6:26).*

One of the many kinds of fowl familiar to the Holy Land is our fine feathered friend, the goose. A wide ranging traveler, as anyone who has seen a "V" formation high overhead can testify, they were known to the Egyptians, and were found in China, India, Europe, and in North America.

Our American Indians even performed goose dances in honor of the bird. In England, a Goose is greatly to be admired as testified to by Tiny Tim in Dicken's "Christmas Carol."

It is indeed a delicious bird, and you can prepare one for yourself and your family:

A FESTIVE ROAST GOOSE

2½ lbs onions, peeled and halved
2 pkgs seasoned bread stuffing
1 tbs poultry seasoning
¼th cup melted butter
1½ cups rich chicken broth
1 goose
lemon juice
Salt & pepper
Plum Sauce

Boil the onions in salted water until tender, about 15 minutes and then coarsley chop. Obtain a large bowl and add the onions to the stuffing mix along with the poultry seasoning, melted butter and the rich chicken broth. Toss until very well mixed.

Take off the neck from the goose and remove the giblets. Wash the bird well, dry thoroughly, and take out as much fat as possible from the cavity. Rub the inside with some lemon juice and sprinkle it with salt and pepper.

Stuff the goose with the dressing and secure the openings with poultry pins and twine. Be certain to tie the legs together and bend the wings under the body.

Use a sharp pointed kitchen knife to gently prick the skin, liberally, especially the breast and the thighs. Try not to make holes in the meat; just the skin.

Roast the bird, uncovered in a 350-F oven for about two hours. Remove the goose from the roasting pan and pour away the fat. Return the goose to the pan and roast two more hours. Again, remove the goose, and pour off the fat, reserving ¼th cup for later use. Return the goose to the pan and continue to roast another ½ hour until the skin is light brown and crisp.

Position the goose on a large serving platter and garnish with water cress. Serve with Plum Sauce.

PLUM SAUCE

1 large can plums
2 tbs reserved goose fat
1½ tbs flour
1 cup Port wine
Dash cinnamon
Dash Tobasco or cayenne pepper

Drain and pit the plums. Crush them and reserve. Heat the goose fat in a small skillet and add the flour, stirring constantly. Cook gently until it is a light brown. Slowly add the wine, and then the plums, cinnamon, and pepper, stirring all the while. Simmer for 5 minutes and serve separately.

"Now that which was prepared for me daily was one ox and six choice sheep; also fowls were prepared for me" (Nehemiah 5:18).

The closest bird to a Rock Cornish Game Hen, that was available for cooks of Bible times was probably the pigeon, which was and is common to the Land of Canaan. Succulent and tasteful, the game hen, like the pigeon can be roasted, broiled, spit-roasted and stuffed to make an attractive and exciting entre.

A Middle East fruit that is very common to Israel is the Tangerine, that wonderful kin of the orange, and blended properly with a juicy game hen, together, they make a dish that will draw nothing but kudos from your guests.

A TANGERINE GAME HEN

2 Rock cornish game hens
2 tangerines, peeled, seeded, and sectioned
6 whole pitted apricots halved
¼th lb butter
Salt
Tangerine sauce
Saffron rice

Wash and dry the game hens, inside and out, and fill the cavities with tangerine pieces and apricot halves.

Close and sew up or fasten the opening, and brush the stuffed birds with butter. Sprinkle lightly with salt and bake at 350-F for about 1½ hours. During the last 30 minutes of cooking, baste them with the tangerine sauce. Halve the cooked hens and serve on mounds of saffron rice with the remaining sauce on the side.

TANGERINE SAUCE

2 tbs cornstarch
2½ cups chicken broth
3 tbs honey
8 pitted prunes, cut in pieces
2 tsp grated tangerine peel
2 tangerines, peeled, seeded and segmented
salt
2 tbs lemon juice

Dissolve the cornstarch in the chicken broth. Add the honey, prunes, and grated tangerine, and pour into a small saucepan. Mix well and let stand for a few minutes.

Then bring to a boil, stirring constantly, and let boil for one minute. Remove from the fire and add the tangerine sections, along with a bit of salt and the lemon juice.

The traders of early times did much to contribute to the dining habits of the world.

As they traveled from land to land and across the seas, they often carried with them live animals and fowl of various kinds from some of the lands they had visited. And some trader, who is now lost in antiquity, once came across southern Asia and the sea of Arabia bearing a brace or more of Chickens.

Their ability to multiply; their eggs, and their rich flesh quickly made them a great favorite of the people of the Holy lands, who learned early to combine them with the fruits of their soil to make many delicious dishes. One of them is:

A JORDAN CHICKEN

1 cup brown olives
1 cup black olives
½ cup green olives
water
2 Cornish Game hens or
2 small fryers, split in half
olive oil
the juice of 2 oranges
1 tbs grated fresh ginger
2 tbs sugar
¼ th cup olive oil
2 garlic cloves, crushed
¼ th cup honey
a pinch of saffron

Put the olives in a saucepan and cover with water. Bring to a boil and reserve.

Split the chickens or the hens in half; wash them and place them in a shallow roasting pan that has been well brushed with olive oil. Squeeze the juice of the oranges over them, and then grate the ginger over them and sprinkle them with the sugar.

In a bowl combine the olive oil, garlic, honey and saffron. Baste the birds with this mixture and broil them carefully for 15 to 20 minutes.

Meanwhile drain the olives, and then place them around the birds. Move them to a 350-F oven for 20 minutes more, and continue to baste them.

Now transfer them to a heated serving platter, and surround them with the olives. Pour the pan juices over them and garnish them with orange wedges.

Serve them with curried rice.

> *"And to bring the first fruits of our ground, and the first fruits of all fruit of all trees, year by year, unto the house of the Lord"*
> *(Nehemiah 10:35).*

One of the first fruits of the land was the lemon. Bright yellow, filled with flavor and rich in Vitamin C, it is a valuable adjunct to good nutrition.

The peoples of all the countries around the Great Sea were well aware of the value of the lemon and used it in a thousand ways. Lemons originated in Asia and migrated rapidly to Spain and Portugal, where they have since become an important export.

The Bible folk were quick to utilize the flavorful and nutritious qualities of the lemon. One way they were combined with an Asia chicken and spices was:

LEMON BARBECUED CHICKEN

2 frying chickens, cut up
Salt & pepper
1 cup butter
the juice of three lemons
1 tbs chopped parsley

Light and form a lovely bed of coals in your barbecue. (Although this dish can also be prepared in your stove broiler). Before placing the chickens on the grill, wash and dry them thoroughly. Combine the butter, melted, parsley, lemon juice. Salt and pepper the chicken pieces, and brush them with the lemon butter. Place them on the barbecue, not too close to the heat and grill them, basting frequently with the lemon butter. Watch them so they cook slowly and come to a nice golden brown. Serve with salad, bread, and white wine.

> *"Thou visitest the earth, and waterest it; Thou greatly enrichest it with the river of God, which is full of water: thou preparest them corn, when Thou hast so provided for it.*
> *Thou waterest the ridges thereof abundantly: Thou settlest the furrows thereof: thou makest it soft with showers: thou blessest the springing thereof" (Psalms 65:9-10).*

Although the above passages from the Bible refer to corn, (which really was wheat), the thanks that David is giving the Lord for his help in making things grow, would certainly include the potatoe, which is also planted in furrows and needs to be watered just like any other vegetable. This recipe is a somewhat novel way of roasting them, and I believe you will enjoy serving it.

FLOWERED POTATOES

4 to 6 nice sized baking potatoes
1 tbs soft butter
3 tbs melted butter or olive oil

Salt
3 tbs bread crumbs
4 tbs grated Cheddar cheese

These could easily have been done amidst hot rocks by a fire, but you can do them in your oven and surprise your guest with an interesting treat. Don't peel the potatoes. Scrub them thoroughly and then place them, one at a time, in a large wooden spoon, and then slice them downward in slices about 1/8th inch thick. The spoon will prevent you from slicing them all the way through. When sliced, drop them in cold water.

When you are ready to roast them, butter a large baking dish or pan and place the potatoes in it, cut side up. Sprinkle them with a little salt, and spoon the melted butter (or Margarine) in between the slices, along with a little olive oil.

Bake them in a 425-F oven and after a few minutes sprinkle them with the bread crumbs.

A little later baste them with some more melted butter and oil and sprinkle with a bit more bread crumbs. Cook them overall for a total of 45 minutes, until they are nicely done.

Sprinkle them with the cheese about 5 minutes before removing them from the oven.

> *"For as the earth bringeth forth her bud, and as the garden causeth the things that are sown in it to spring forth; so the Lord GOD will cause righteousness and praise to spring forth before all the nations" (Isaiah 61:11).*

Leeks are mentioned a number of time in the Bible. (Numbers 11:5 especially notes them). And they are certainly one of the more useful vegetables that GOD caused to spring forth from the soil.

According to most researchers, Leeks are native to the Mediterranean region, and were eaten by Egyptian, Roman and Greek gourmets. It has been said that the Roman despot, Nero ate them, because he believed they would improve his "singing" voice. The French call Leeks the "Asparagus of the poor," and a most interesting way to prepare them, and a somewhat glamorous way, is to braise; a dish that is quite appropriately called:

BRAISED LEEKS GOURMET

3 or 4 large leeks, well washed and with the green tops removed
1 onion, sliced
2 stalks celery, sliced lengthwise
2 carrots, sliced lengthwise
8 slices bacon
1 cup beef bullion
1 bay leaf
Salt
Pepper
1 tsp cornstarch
water

Blanch the leeks and celery by immersing them in enough cold water to cover along with 1 tbs taragon vinegar.

Bring the water to a boil, and then remove and drain well. Now put 4 slices of beef bacon in the bottom of a shallow baking dish, and lay the leeks and celery on top. Cover them with the onion slices and the carrot slices, and sprinkle them with salt and pepper. Add the bay leaf. Now cover them with the remaining 4 slices of bacon.

Pour undiluted beef boullion over and cover with a piece of well buttered wax paper.

Braise in a pre-heated oven at 350-F for about 1½ hours. Remove the vegetables and keep warm. Dissolve the cornstarch in just enough cold water, and add to the juices in the baking pan. Heat on top of the stove until slightly thickened and glossy.

Pour this sauce over the vegetables in a serving dish and garnish with fresh parsley if so desired.

> *"And the Lord GOD prepared a gourd, and made it to come up over Jonah, that it might be a shadow over his head to deliver him from his grief. So Jonah was exceedingly glad of the gourd"* (Jonah 4:6).

The Lord not only gave Jonah a gourd, he presented the whole world with them. Little ones, big ones, all sizes and shapes. Not only were they used for food, but some of them were dried and used to carry other foods, and sometimes water. Today, they are just as delicious to sup on as they were in

Biblical times, and of the thousand and one ways they can be prepared, I find this recipe one of the best.

A MEDLEY OF GOURDS

3 crookneck squash, sliced
3 zuchinni, sliced
3 pattypan squash, sliced
2 large onions, sliced
1 10-oz) pkg frozen green beans
Water
2 green tomatoes, sliced
½ tsp oregano
2 tbs chopped parsley
Salt, pepper
Juice of 1 lemon
2 tbs salad oil

If you are a squash lover you will:
Combine the squashes, onion, and thawed green beans in a saucepan. Add one inch of water, cover and let steam for 20 minutes. Add the tomato slices and let cook for three minutes longer. Drain, and add the oregano, parsley, and salt and pepper to taste. Sprinkle with lemon juice and olive oil and toss lightly.

> *"And Jacob sod pottage: And Esau came from the field, and he was faint: And Esau said to Jacob, Feed me, I pray thee with that same red pottage; for I am faint: therefore was his name called Edom....Then Jacob gave Esau bread and pottage of lentils; and he did eat and drink, and rose up and went his way" (Genesis 25:29-30, 34).*

Lentils: In Hebrew ADASHIM. A beanlike plant much esteemed in the East as an article of food.

As indicated, lentils were and still are a very important part of Middle Eastern fare, and if you happen to have some left-over Lamb in your refrigerator, here is a Biblelike way of using it to prepare a very savory dish.

BIBLICAL LENTILS

2 cups dried lentils
1 onion
A bay leaf
1 tbs salt
1 tbs chopped parsley
2 cups cooked lamb, cut in chunks
2 tbs butter or margarine

Here again, one would need an earthenware pot, preferably one with a tight fitting lid. First of all; put the lentils in a large saucepan; cover them with water, add the onion, bay leaf and the salt and simmer for at least 45 minutes. Drain the lentils and save the liquid. Spoon about 1/3rd of the lentils into the bean pot and add a layer of lamb. Repeat the process ending with a topping of lentils. Pour in the reserved liquid and bake for 1 hour in a 350-F oven.

"Therefore, thou shalt speak unto them this word; thus saith the Lord God of Israel, every bottle shall be filled with wine" (Jeremiah 13:12).

The Bible indicates that when the Ark finally settled on Mount Ararat, and the flood water receded, one of the first projects Noah accomplished was to plant a grape vine.

Wine was not regarded as an intoxicant by our ancestors; rather as something to be honored and used to clear one's palate and flavor foods.

Basically, the same rules apply today. The proper use of a good wine can raise a dish from peasantry to nobility!

WINED HALIBUT STEAKS

4 halibut steaks
1 cup Chablis wine
Salt & pepper
1 cup Matzo Meal
½ cup butter
2 tbs butter
1 onion, chopped

½ sweet red pepper, chopped
½ sweet green pepper, chopped
1 tsp curry powder
lemon juice

Let the fish steaks marinate in the wine for 15 minutes, and then salt and pepper them, and then dredge them with the matzo meal.

Saute the steaks gently in the butter and then place in a casserole.

In a saucepan, melt the additional butter, add the chopped onion, and the chopped peppers.

Gently saute until vegetables are tender. Add the curry powder, and mix well. Continue to cook for a few more minutes. Add the wine from the marinade along with the lemon juice, and bring to a boil, stirring all the while.

Pour the sauce over the fish steaks and bake in a 450-F oven for 10 minutes, or until the fish is tender. Pour the sauce left over in the casserole over the pieces of fish when serving.

"A land of wheat and barley, and vines, and fig trees and pomegranetes; a land of olive oil and honey" (Deuteronomy 8:8).

Historically, ducks are not mentioned in the Bible, but the slaves of the Pharaohs were very familiar with them, and savored them. Their existence was recorded in the Egyptian hieroglyphics.

The Romans used figs to fatten their ducks and often used wine to add additional flavor.

There are some 125 species of ducks, ranging all over the world. Those consumed by the Egyptians and the peoples of the Holy Land were probably salt water ducks, although there is some evidence that fresh water ducks existed in Canaan.

In any event, they can easily be procured these days, and one of the most glamorous ways to cook and serve duck is:

A NILE DUCK

2 dozen fresh figs
Dry Sack Port wine
1 5-lb duckling
canned figs
celery leaves

canned apricots
Honey
Apricot halves, heated
orange segments

The day before put the fresh figs in a jar along with enough Port wine to cover and let them soak overnite.

On the day of preparation, wash and dry the duckling thoroughly and remove the wing tips and the neck. Dry well and rub the inside with some lemon juice. Stuff the bird with the canned apricots and the canned figs, along with some celery leaves.

When ready, put the fruit-stuffed duck in a 350-F oven for ½ hour, preferably in an earthware baking dish.

Remove the duck and set aside and pour off all the fat from the dish, and replace with the Port wine in which the fresh figs have been soaking. Reserve the figs. Place the duck back in the oven in the dish, and bake for another hour, basting often with the wine and drippings in the dish.

Now add the marinated figs, the orange slices, and the apricot halves to the dish and bake the contents for another ½ hour. Fifteen minutes before the duck is done, brush well with honey, and do not baste again.

Serve on a heated platter surrounded by the heated fruit. Skim off the fat from the pan juices, and serve separately.

> *"And it came to pass, when David was come to Mahanaim, that Shobi, the son of Nahash of Rabbath of the children of Ammon, and Machir, the son of Ammiel of Lo-Debar, and Barzillai the Gileadite of Rogelim brought beds and basons, and earthen vessels, and wheat and barley and flour, and parched corn and beans, and lentils and parched pulse" (II Samuel 17:27-28).*

My old family Bible Dictionary says that beans are a native of Palestine, Syria, and Asia Minor. That they blossomed from January to March, when planted in November and gathered in February. Both the green pod and ripe beans, boiled with oil and garlic are commonly used by persons of all classes.

There are several kinds, some of which are fed to horses. We know that when the people of the Exodus left Egypt, they took with them cattle, unleavened bread dough, pots and jars, and, of course, all the recipes the ladies of the caravan could hold in their heads. A modern day version of one that probably originated in ancient times is called:

EGYPTIAN GREEN BEANS

1 large onion, chopped
2 tbs olive oil
1 tbs butter
1½ lbs cubed lamb
1 (6-oz) can tomato paste
1 (15-oz) can tomato sauce
½ cup white wine
Salt & pepper
2 (10-oz) pkgs frozen green beans
2 to 3 cups water
Dash of garlic powder
Dash of cumin

At Succoth, or any of the other watering places where the wandering Tribes of Israel camped to rest and graze their flocks, they may well have enjoyed watching their cook saute the onions in olive oil until they were brown.

Then she added the lamb cubes and gently browned them on all sides. The tomato paste was added along with the tomato sauce and the wine. Seasoned with salt and pepper, the mixture was covered until the meat was almost done. Then the beans, garlic powder and cumin were added and the dish was simmered for another 20 to 30 minutes.

This served 6 people.

Chapter Three

On the Exodus Trail

The only event in modern times that can favorably compare in size and mobility to the "Exodus" was the "D" day invasion of Europe on June 6th, 1944.

At the time of the Exodus, more than 600,000 men, in addition to women and children crossed out of Egypt, into the wilderness. All together they totaled more than a million people, who, with their herds of cattle, sheep and goats, and their fowls, and panikins of unleavened bread and spices crossed the Red Sea and went onward into the wilderness of the Arabian peninsula to wander for more than 40 years, before reaching their goal, "The Land of Milk and Honey": Canaan.

This fantastic journey was all made possible in the beginning by the plagues that the LORD visited upon Egypt, which resulted in the freedom of the children of Israel.

> *"And he, (The Pharaoh) called for Moses and Aaron by night and said, rise up and get you forth from among my people, both ye and the children of Israel; and go serve the LORD, as Ye have said.*
>
> *"Also take your flocks and your herds, as Ye have said and be gone; and bless me also" (Exodus 12:31-32).*

What a great general and leader Moses must have been to lead all those people and their flocks and herds across hundreds of miles of harsh desert and mountains, and all the while kept them fed, watered, and at the same time, disciplined and prepared for their final arrival in the Holy Land.

THE FIRST MIRACLE ON THE TRAIL

"And it came to pass, that at even the Quails came up and covered the camp; and in the morning the dew lay round about the host" (Exodus 16:13).

It wasn't long after the start of the Exodus that more than a little grumbling appeared amongst the Children of Israel. After all, the life they led in Egypt was pretty well ordered, and they were well fed. But as the Exodus progressed, it soon became apparent that food was going to be hard to obtain; and it was!

By the time they reached the "Wilderness of Sin," on the shores of the Red Sea, now known as the "Plain of El Kaa," they were in sore need.

It was there that the Lord granted them two great miracles to augment their meager diet.

The first was the Miracle of the Quails.

The seasonal time at this point in the Exodus was spring when great flocks of birds leave Africa and begin their annual migration Northward. Quails and many other birds have to cross the Red Sea, and it is only logical that they are exhausted after that first long leg of their journey, so they stop to rest on the "Plains of El Kaa," before beginning the next stage of their trek.

Tired and weak, they are easy prey, and even today, the Arabs of this area catch them by hand.

In addition to Quail, more than 360 kinds of birds are to be found in Palestine; 26 are found only there.

Birds are mentioned in 45 of the books of the Bible.

Among the game birds considered clean and therefore acceptable for eating were Doves, Hens, Partridge, Pigeons, Sparrows, Turtle Doves and Geese.

Now, if there is a good hunter in your Tribe, you might try some of these recipes, I have gathered to grace your table.

EXODUS QUAIL

3/4ths cup butter
4½ tbs olive oil

12 small whole white onions, peeled
1/8th tsp fresh ground black pepper
3 cans chicken broth
1 mediun can button mushrooms, drained
12 Quail, about 5-oz each
2 tbs butter
3 tbs EACH butter and olive oil
1 can pitted ripe olives
2 tbs minced onion
2 tbs minced carrot
2 tbs minced celery
2 sprigs chopped parsley
1 bay leaf
1/8th tsp thyme
1 clove garlic, minced
1 tbs tomato sauce
3 tbs cornstarch
½ cup dry white wine
melted butter
12 large bread triangles

I'm quite certain the children of Israel didn't have all these goodies with them on the trail, but we can hope that they did prepare this lovely dish when they were firmly ensconced in Jerusalem.

Heat 1½ tbs EACH butter and olive oil in a skillet. Add the whole onions and saute them for 10 minutes, shaking the skillet so the onions brown lightly and evenly. Be careful to keep the onions whole and nicely shaped.

Drain off the fat. Sprinkle the onions with pepper and add one can of chicken broth. Cover and simmer for 15 minutes or until onions are almost tender. Remove the onions with a slotted spoon and reserve the chicken broth. Add 2 tbs butter to the skillet and heat until the butter stops foaming. Add the drained mushrooms and cook and stir them over medium heat until they are lightly browned on all sides. Remove the mushrooms and reserve. Add 3 tbs EACH butter and olive oil to the drippings in the skillet, heat. Now add the Quail, a few at a time, and brown them. In a large casserole, arrange the Quail, browned onions and mushrooms, along with the olives.

In the skillet used for frying the Quail, add the minced onion, carrot, celery, parsley, bay leaf, thyme, garlic, tomato sauce and the remaining 2 cans of chicken broth.

Add the liquid reserved from the braised whole onions. Bring to a boil; cover and simmer for 30 minutes.

Blend the cornstarch with the wine and stir into the simmering sauce. Cook and stir until the sauce comes to a boil and is clear.

Continue cooking for another 5 minutes, skimming off any fat that surfaces. Strain the sauce and pour it over the Quail in the casserole. Cover lightly, using foil if necessary, and bake in a 350-F oven for 30 minutes. Meanwhile gently saute the bread triangles in melted butter until they are crisp and brown. Serve the Quail on the bread triangles, and spoon some of the sauce over them. Serve the remaining sauce separately.

THE SECOND MIRACLE ON THE TRAIL

"MANNA"

"And when the dew that lay was gone up, behold, upon the face of the Wilderness there lay a small round thing, as small as the hoar frost on the ground.

And when the children of Israel saw it, they said to one another, it is Manna: for they wist not what it was. And Moses said unto them, this is the bread which the Lord hath given you to eat" (Exodus 16:14-15).

Manna: "The bread of heaven." A miracle, which the skeptics deny? Perhaps. And yet there is more than enough evidence to indicate that some form of the "Bread of Heaven" has existed down through the ages.

In 1483, a Pilgrim, making his way to Sinai wrote that in the whole region of Sinai the bread of heaven was to be found and he indicated it was gathered by both the monks and the Arabs and that it was preserved and often sold to the Pilgrims passing that way.

"And the children of Israel did eat Manna for 40 years, until they came to a land inhabited; they did eat Manna until they came unto the borders of the Land of Canaan" (Exodus 16:35).

Since Moses defined Manna as bread, the term, "Manna from Heaven," has indicated bread and has become synonymous with good fortune and good eating. In almost every language bread is known as the staff of life. Bread has been important since pre-historic times. In the beginning, it was surely unleavened.

The discovery of leavening is credited to the Egyptians who were famous for their breads, in Biblical times. The Exodus travelers were forced to eat unleavened bread in the beginning.

> *"And they baked unleavened cakes of the dough which they brought forth out of Egypt, for it was not leavened: because they were thrust out of Egypt, and could not tarry, neither had they prepared for themselves any victual" (Exodus 12:39).*

Since that time, however, people have enjoyed bread both leavened and unleavened. It is a basic food, and its varieties bear the imprints of every culture in the world. It is indeed a blessing of the Lord God!

> *"And the people took their dough, before it was leavened, their kneading doughs being bound up in their clothes upon their shoulders" (Exodus 12:34).*

The Hebrews were forced to leave Egypt in such a hurry, they were unable to take any leavened bread with them. Thus, the very first bread they ate on the trail was unleavened. Since then, unleavened bread has become very much a part of the Hebrew heritage:

> *"Seven days thou shalt eat unleavened bread, and in the seventh day shall be a feast to the LORD" (Exodus 13:6).*

Unleavened bread has been a staple for most of the lands of the Middle East as well as Asia for a great many years. As a matter of fact; it is still a principle item of food for lands stretching from India, across the Red Sea to Africa and on up to the Mediterranean.

This recipe is traditionally eaten at the celebration of the "Passover."

MATZO BREAD

3 eggs
½ tsp salt
¾ cup chicken broth
1 cup matzo meal
⅓ cup cake meal
4 tbs melted chicken fat

Beat the eggs and salt together, and stir in the chicken broth alternately with the matzo meal and the cake meal. (Note: Cake meal can be obtained at stores specializing in Jewish foods.) Add the melted fat. Mound and place in a baking pan that has been well greased, and bake in a 350-F oven for about 30 minutes, until nicely browned.

In every sense, the men, women, and children of the Exodus were pioneers. Like the hardy souls that crossed the great American prairies, the Exodus people traveled slowly and had to guard themselves every moment in order to survive. And like our early pioneers, the people of Israel, headed for the promised land, had to learn to make-do with shelter, living habits, and especially with food. This is a bread recipe that is today noted for its similarity to that used by our latter day pioneers, and it is certain to have much in common with the bread that was baked on the long, long trek of the children of Israel!

"A WAGON TRAIN BREAD"

2½ to 3 cups all-purpose flour
1 pkg dry yeast
1¼ cups water
2 tbs honey, or 1 tbs sugar
Some cornmeal

Using a fairly large bowl, mix 1 cup of the flour and the yeast. Some cooks prefer to try out the yeast in some warm water before using, but it isn't always necessary.

Using a saucepan, heat the water, honey, and/or sugar, and the salt until barely warm. Add to the flour and yeast mixture and beat with an electric hand mixer for about 30 seconds. Then increase the speed of the mixer to high and beat for another 3 or 4 minutes. Now add enough remaining flour to make a soft dough. Shape into a ball and place in a well greased bowl, cover, and place in a draft-free area and let rise until it has doubled, which should take about 1 hour.

Grease well, a large baking pan, sprinkle with the cornmeal, and place the dough in it. Cover and let rise again until it has doubled in size. This should take about 45 to 50 minutes.

Bake at 400-F for 45 minutes.

Remove from the pan and let cool. If carefully sliced while still warm and well coated with butter this makes a tasty morsel!

> *"As the partridge sitteth on eggs, and hatcheth them not; so he that getteth riches, and not by right, shall leave them in the midst of his days, and at his end shall be a fool" (Jeremiah 17:11).*

The above allegory does not give much credit to the partridge, but it does indicate that the bird was known in Bible lands, and, if I am any judge of gourmet eating, I'm sure the hunters of that time enjoyed their "bag" of partridges just as much then as we do today.

A simple way to prepare them, after they have been well plucked and drawn and cleaned, is to braise them.

This is easy to make, and it will guarantee you a most pleasant pheasant supper.

BRAISED PHEASANT

1 pheasant, cut into serving pieces
¼ cup butter
¼ cup lemon juice
¼ cup vinegar
1 tsp garlic salt
½ tsp cayenne pepper
½ tsp chopped onion
2 tbs chopped fresh parsley

Brown the pheasant pieces in butter in the skillet. Remove from the pan, and add seasonings to the pan drippings, and cook for about 3 minutes.

Return the pheasant to the pan, and cover. Cover and cook over medium heat for one hour, basting frequently with the sauce.

> *"And their father Israel, said unto them, if it must be so now, do this; take of the best fruits in the land in your vessels, and carry down the man a present, a little balm, and a little honey, spices and myrrh, nuts and almonds" (Genesis 43:11).*

Nuts of all sorts were freely available to the Mediterranean lands. Almonds, walnuts, pistachios, and surely pine nuts. Peanuts, however, were not native to Europe and Africa until the Spanish returned with them from their conquests in the New World, and introduced them to Europe, Africa, and Asia, where they became immensely popular.

In any event, I have decided to take some liberties and dedicate this next African recipe to a deeply religious gentleman and a peanut farmer, the Honorable Jimmy Carter, the 39th President of these United States.

"PEANUT CHICKEN A LA CARTER"

A (5 to 6 lb) roasting chicken, cut into serving pieces
1 cup finely ground peanuts
1 cup milk
1 tbs salt
1 tbs grated fresh ginger
½ cup peanut oil
1 cup finely chopped onions
1 large can peeled tomatoes
½ cup tomato sauce
1 tsp finely minced garlic
½ tsp cayenne pepper
½ tsp white pepper
6 cups boiling water
2 whole canned Anaheim chilies, chopped
1 cup peanut butter (chunk style)
2 cans Okra
6 hard cooked eggs

AT THE WHITE HOUSE, YOU WOULD:
Wash and clean the chicken and then dry with paper towels. Then heat the oil in a deep, heavy skillet; dip the chicken pieces in the milk and then into the ground peanuts, and place them in the oil. Carefully cook until they are golden brown. Start with the dark meat pieces followed in a few minutes by the white meat pieces. Doing this will make all the pieces come out nicely browned and cooked to a turn. Remove the chicken parts individually as they are browned, and place them on a warm platter to keep warm.

Retain ¼ cup of the cooking oil and discard the remainder. To the retained oil, add the onions, and cook until they are soft, but not browned. Stir in the brown bits clinging to the pot. This should take about 5 minutes.

Now add the canned tomatoes which have been drained and chopped rather coarsley. Also add the tomato sauce, garlic, ginger, cayenne pepper, and the white pepper.

Bring this mixture to a boil, constantly stirring. Reduce the heat and cook slowly for about 5 minutes. Now add the boiling water a little at a time, and add the chilies. Return the chicken to the skillet along with it's juices and simmer uncovered, for about 15 minutes. Turn the chicken pieces, from time to time to keep them evenly coated with the sauce.

Stir in the peanut butter and the okra and cover and simmer gently for one hour, until the chicken is tender.

Add the hard cooked eggs and cook for another 5 minutes.

Serve this stew in a nice big heated bowl, along with chopped peanuts, diced ripe melons, which have been well chilled, a chopped tomato salad, and some fried banana halves.

"The sleep of a laboring man is sweet, whether he eat little or much" (Ecclesiastes 5:12).

As I indicated earlier, chicken originated in the jungles of Southeast Asia. There, amidst the jungle plants and the bamboo thickets he strutted and crowed much like any other jungle animal. In any event, probably around 1400 B.C., some trader-hunter captured some of the breed, and island hopping his way homeward, brought the bird across southern Asia, India, thence north to the Holy Lands, and finally to Europe.

It was in the early 1600s that the chicken finally made its way to America. Interestingly enough, in the beginning they were raised for their feathers which were used to stuff pillows. However, they soon developed another use, and that was a taste for their savory flesh. And it wasn't long before they became a staple in nearly everyone's diet.

This recipe is an easy way to prepare chicken, and yet I find it most agreeable.

CHICKEN CITRUS

½ cup soft butter or margarine
½ cup fresh lemon juice
2 small fryers cut in pieces, (or cut in half)
Salt and pepper

Clean the chickens and either cut them up or just halve them. Set aside while you prepare the lemon butter.

Simply combine the softened butter and the lemon juice. (You can use more lemon juice if you desire a more tart taste.)

Now, dry the chickens with paper towels, lightly salt and pepper them, and put them under the broiler.

Brush them well with some of the lemon butter and turn the broiler on. Caution: Don't turn the broiler up to high, and don't get the birds too close to the flame.

Do them gently, and baste with the lemon butter, and you will end up with a most savory dinner.

You can also do these chickens on a barbecue grill, using the same procedure, and they will be just as lovely to eat.

Garnish the plates with something green, some french fried potatoes, and some lemon slices.

> *"And the men are shepherds, for their trade hath been to feed cattle; and they have brought their flocks, and their herds, and all that they have" (Genesis 46:32).*

Cattle were of great importance to the Hebrews.

One of their first tasks, when they were placed in bondage in Egypt, was to herd the cattle in the Land of Goshen. And when they left Egypt, they took their herds with them. Moses made a special point of this, when he bargained for their freedom with the Pharaoh.

> *"And Moses said: we will go with our young and with our old, with our sons and with our daughters, with our flocks, and with our herds will we go; for we must hold a feast unto the LORD" (Exodus 10:9).*

> *"Our cattle also shall go with us; there shall not an hoof be left behind; for thereof must we take to serve the LORD our GOD" (Exodus 10:26).*

In fact Cattle were of such importance that during the 40 years of wandering in the Wilderness, it took more than a little planning on Moses' part to insure there was pasturage at each stopping place.

And if you have ever enjoyed a beautifully prepared steak, or a wonderful slice of English Roast Beef, or a dainty Filet Mignon; not to mention many other beef cuts, you are sure to know whereof I write.

I rather doubt the traveling Children of Israel knew much about the cuts I have just mentioned, but they did have ways of cooking their beef, some of which have come down to us through the corridors of time.

BARBECUED SHORT RIBS

3 lbs beef short ribs
1 cup tomato juice
1 tsp salt
½ tsp pepper
1 clove garlic, minced
1 onion, finely chopped
1 tsp dry mustard
2 tbs honey
½ cup red wine
1 tsp Worcestershire sauce
1/8 tsp Tobasco

Some people like to use a meat tenderizer when preparing short ribs. If you do, use it according to the label on the bottle.

In any event, combine all the remaining ingredients in a saucepan and bring to a low boil and then reduce the heat and simmer over low heat for about 15 minutes.

Be sure to stir as it is heating, else it may burn.

Place the ribs on the barbecue grill about 5 inches away from the source of heat and cook for 25 to 30 minutes, basting frequently with the sauce.

Serve this with large chunks of Garlic French bread, a crisp green tossed salad, some Burgundy wine, and some foil wrapped barbecued potatoes.

> *"And he took butter and milk and the calf which he had dressed, and sat it before them; and he stood by them under the tree, and they did eat" (Genesis 18:8).*

True veal, which is available in the spring is young beef from four to fourteen weeks of age. Like a young lamb it is often served in rather large pieces, either barbecued, roasted, or cut into smaller chops and steaks. In southern Germany, of course, it is often scalloped.

Historically, it has been regarded with relish in all the nations bordering on the "Great Sea," especially by the Greeks and Romans, as well as those denizens of the Holy Lands. As indicated in the passage from the Bible above, however, it was generally reserved for very special occasions, such as the visit of the Lord and his angels.

A Middle Eastern way to prepare veal shoulder steaks and one that can be prepared with many variations is common to the lands that were once part of the Golden Scimitar:

DILLED VEAL SHOULDER STEAKS

Flour
Salt & pepper
6 veal shoulder steaks
2 tbs beef suet
1 cup chopped onions
2 cups beef stock
2 garlic cloves, crushed
1 cup Bhulgar, or Kasha
1 bunch asparagus
1 cup Rosé wine
1 cup dairy sour cream
1 tbs dillweed

Dredge the veal steaks in the mixture of the flour, salt and pepper, and then brown them gently in the melted suet. Remove the veal to a flame-proof casserole.

In the pan used to brown the veal, gently simmer the onions, beef stock, the wine and the garlic. Add to the veal steaks, cover and simmer for 1½ hours until the veal is tender.

Meanwhile cook the Bulghar according to the directions on the package. In another pan cook the asparagus until tender.

Remove the veal steaks, when finished and keep warm. Strain the juices from the casserole, and that from the asparagus and blend well. Add the sour cream, the dill weed, and the salt and pepper to taste.

Combine some of this sauce with the Bulghar and mound it in the center of a large platter. Surround with the veal steaks and garnish with the asparagus.

Serve the remaining sauce separately.

> *"And Abraham ran unto the herd and fetch a calf tender and good, and gave it to a young man, and he hasted to dress it"*
> *(Genesis 18:7).*

Veal, like the lamb a symbol of innocence and purity. Fed with milk, white in color, soft in texture, veal is known and desired from the North to the South and the East to the West.

Bear in mind that when the children of Israel slaughtered a calf, they were really making a personal sacrifice, because very often that meant a future sire would be lost to the herd.

However, in more modern times, whether it be an Italian Scallopini, a Greek style dish, a Vienese Weiner Schnitzel, it is considered by gourmets the world over as a meat much to be desired.

In several countries, they add some green olives, a bit of wine, and a touch of garlic to create veal unexcelled!

ABRAHAM'S VEAL CUTLETS

6 tbs butter
6 lean veal cutlets
¼ cup minced onion
⅓ cup minced beef bologne
¼ cup burgundy wine
½ cup pitted green olives
½ tsp minced garlic

Melt the butter in a thick, heavy skillet.

Add the cutlets and gently brown on both sides. Please do not use a very high heat as all this does is toughen the meat! Now add the wine, onion, and bologne to the cutlets. Cover the skillet and cook on very low heat until the meat is tender, turning once.

Add the olives and garlic; cover again and cook until the cutlets are nice and tender.

Arrange the cutlets on a platter and pour the sauce over them.

> *"In the tenth day of this month, they shall take to them, every man a lamb, according to the house of their fathers, a lamb for a house" (Exodus 12:3).*

The lamb was considered a symbol of innocence and as we all know, Christ was called "The Lamb of God" by John the Baptist.

Although it probably originated in Asia as an off-shoot of the great Big Horn Sheep, it migrated early in time to the Middle East, where it was savored by the ancient Greeks and Romans, and since most of the early Israelites were shepherds, it soon became of major importance.

Today, it is probably the most popular meat of the area and is served ground, skewered, and roasted as well as with vegetables.

One way it might have been served at King Solomon's table is flavored with Saffron, a spice of which Solomon was exceedingly fond.

LAMB SAFFRON STEW

2 lbs lamb stew meat
2 tbs butter
1 medium onion, chopped
1½ tbs flour
1½ cups water
¼ tsp powdered Saffron
1 2-inch stick cinnamon
1 tsp salt
1/8 tsp pepper
¾ cup large dried prunes
2 tsp grated orange peel
2 tsp sugar

King Solomon's chef might have suggested that you cut the lamb into 1½ inch cubes and lightly brown them in butter.

Remove the browned meat with a slotted spoon and reserve.

Add the onion to the drippings in the pan and cook gently until tender, but not browned. Stir in flour and cook until well browned. Stir from time to time and watch carefully so the mixture does not burn! Return the meat to the pot and add the water and bring to a boil, stirring until smooth. Stir in the Saffron, cinnamon, salt and pepper, and cover and reduce the heat, and simmer for 1½ hours, adding water if the stew becomes too thick. Meanwhile put the prunes in warm water and let stand for one hour. Drain and add to the stew. Stir in the orange peel and the sugar and heat thoroughly.

Remove the cinnamon stick and serve.

You'll love it and so would have Solomon!

About the only reference in the Bible to onions is in the book of Numbers, (Chapter 11, vs. 5), but whether or not you are a part of an "Exodus" or have found your "Promised Land," you will enjoy these delicious onions, quite probably prepared much as they were in earlier times. They are easy to prepare and involve only the following:

GRILL ROASTED ONIONS

Unpeeled onions
Butter or margarine
Salt and pepper
Sugar

A wandering nomad might have in his pack some yellow cooking onions, or some sweet red onions, or even some large white cooking onions. In any case he would wash them, and placed them on a spot over glowing coals of charcoal. He would roast them for about an hour, not too close to the coals, turning them often to make certain they roasted evenly.

When ready to eat, he would strip off the skins, or perhaps cut them in half and dress them with a little butter or margarine, some salt and pepper, and a dash of sugar. All alone, he would eat two, just for himself. And you should allow just about that for your Nomadic guests. (Don't forget yourself!)

> *"Take thou also unto thee wheat, and barley and beans, and lentils and millet, and fitches, and put them in one vessel, and make thee bread thereof, according to the number of the days that thou shalt lie upon thy side, three hundred and ninety days shalt thou eat thereof" (Ezekiel 4:9).*

Beans were found in Bronze Age deposits, dating back as far as 3,000 years before Christ. Historians have noted that they were grown by the Greeks, Romans, and the Egyptians, certainly making it plausible that they were well-known to the people of Israel.

One simple way to prepare a very tasty bean dish uses pimientos, which are very common in the Middle East.

JERUSALEM WHITE BEANS

1½ cups white pea beans, washed and drained
6 cups water
1 cup chicken stock
1 cup fresh tomatoes, finely chopped
1 onion, finely chopped
1 clove garlic, minced

¾ cup butter melted (or margarine)
4 pimientos, cut in strips

This dish is very colorful and goes well with lamb, or chicken. It will indeed enhance any dinner as well as please any palate.

Cover the beans with water, and bring to a boil for 2 minutes. Cover the pot and let them stand for at least one hour.

Then return the beans to the fire and bring again to a boil; lower the heat and let simmer until they are tender.

One may have to add a bit more water from time to time to keep them from burning.

Mix in the tomatoes, chicken stock, onion, garlic, butter and cook in a pre-heated 350-F oven for about 1 hour. Uncover, add the pimiento strips and cook 30 minutes longer. This will make 4 to 6 servings.

"Prove thy servants, I beseech thee, ten days: and let them give us pulse to eat and water to drink" (Daniel 1:12).

Pulse: In Hebrew: *Zerohim,* "to scatter, to sow."
A general name for peas, beans, and such kinds of garden sauce.

Although beans were not specifically mentioned in the Bible, we do know they were grown in that part of the world by all the people that lived there and they are certainly one of the blessings given us by the fruitful earth, on instruction from the Lord.

Most people from every land make them a major part of their daily fare for, as the saying goes, "they stick to the ribs and give you something to work on!"

CHEESED WHITE BEANS

2 cups white beans
2 quarts water
6 cups chicken broth
Salt
½ cups onions, sliced
3 tbs butter
2 tbs parsley, chopped
2 tbs butter or margarine
2 tbs flour

1 cup Half & Half
½ tsp salt
2 tbs grated white Cheddar cheese
4 tbs honey

An Israelite mother would have put the beans, covered with water on the dying coals of the fire just before retiring and let them come to a slow boil for about 2 minutes, and then set them aside to rest for the night. In the morning, she would have drained them well, and added them to the chicken broth.

Then she would have added the salt, and put the beans on the fire to let them simmer until they were tender. In another pot or pan she would have cooked the onions in oil until tender and then added them to the beans along with the chopped parsley and the honey.

Then mixing the flour with the milk, she would have heated it slowly until thickened.

Add this to the beans and top it all with grated cheese. Cover it and bake in a 300-F oven for about 45 minutes.

Try this with your next roast leg of Lamb!

"Thou madest him to have dominion over the works of thy hands; thou hast put all things under his feet."

"All sheep and oxen, yea, and the beasts of the field." (Psalms 8:6-7).

This particular recipe originally came from Iraq, a land, which along with Syria and Jordan borders on the land of Canaan.

All the peoples of these lands ate much the same foods; sheep, cattle, barley, wheat, corn, and vegetables. Preparation methods were often somewhat different according to their native bent, but by and large the end product was a good food, well prepared, and worthy of an educated palate. Not to mention it's ability to help one survive in the wilderness!

PERSIAN MEATBALLS

½ lb ground lamb
½ cup minced onion
2 tbs olive oil
¼ cup water

½ tsp ground ginger
¼ tsp tumeric
¼ tsp garlic powder
½ tsp salt
½ tsp chopped parsley
Potato dough
1 beaten egg
1 cup oil
1 cup Peta bread crumbs
Tomato Dip

Gently saute the meat in the olive oil, breaking it up, until it is lightly browned. Then add the onion for a few minutes until it is tender. Now add the water, ginger, tumeric, garlic powder, salt and chopped parsley and let simmer for 10 minutes. Let it cool enough to handle and then form into very small balls, using about a half teaspoon of the mixture for each ball.

Shape the potato dough around each ball, rolling it to make a symetrical ball.

Dip each ball in the beaten egg, and then roll in the Peta bread crumbs. (These are easily made; just dry them in a moderate oven, let cool, and place in your blender.) Cook the crumbed balls in hot olive oil until they are golden all over. Drain on paper towels and serve with a Tahineh, or a tomato dip.

TOMATO DIP (FOR IRAQ MEATBALLS)

1 can tomato paste
1 tsp lemon juice
¼ tsp salt
¼ tsp pepper
½ tsp garlic powder
½ tsp ginger
A dash cayenne pepper
A dash cumin
1 tsp sugar

Blend all the ingredients thoroughly and chill slightly.

POTATO DOUGH FOR IRAQUI MEATBALLS

2 cups instant potatoes
2 cups peta bread crumbs
1 tsp salt
2 tbs olive oil
2 eggs
2 cups hot water

Put together the instant potato, crumbs and the salt. Make a well in the center and add the oil, eggs and water. Stir until well blended and has formed a soft dough. Use to coat the meatballs.

> "Turn ye, and take your journey, and go to the mount of the Amorites, and unto all the places nigh thereunto, in the plain, in the hills, and in the vale, and in the South, and by the seaside, to the land of the Canaanites, and unto Lebanon, unto the great river, the river Euphrates" (Deuteronomy 1:7).

Among the nations that border the Holy Land are Lebanon and Syria. Whatever their differences, they all share a love of finely prepared lamb. One of the more interesting ways to prepare it is called "Kibbeh," which is generally regarded as the national dish of both countries.

KIBBEH

2 cups fine Bulghar
2 lbs finely ground lamb
1 large onion, grated
1½ tsp salt
½ tsp fresh ground black pepper
¼ tsp allspice
4 tbs butter
¼ cup Sesame Seeds
1 cup pine nuts, shelled
1 lb lamb shoulder meat ground
1 cup onion, finely chopped
½ tsp EACH salt and ground cinnamon

¼ tsp EACH allspice and black pepper
2 tbs chopped fresh mint
2 tbs EACH olive oil and melted butter

IF YOU HAVE NEVER TASTED THIS DISH, YOU HAVE MISSED A DELIGHT!

Soak the fine ground bulghar in ice water for 10 minutes. Drain it and squeeze it dry through a towel or some cheesecloth. Combine it with the ground lamb, the onion, salt and pepper, and the allspice. Knead it, just as you would dough, dipping your hands in cold water, until the mixture is smooth and elastic. Set aside.

In the butter gently brown the pine nuts, and then add them to the ground shoulder of lamb meat, and cook for about 10 minutes. Then add the onions, salt and cinnamon, allspice, and black pepper. Remove from the heat and add the chopped mint. Now butter a shallow baking pan. Press ⅓ of the basic Kibbeh mixture into the bottom of the pan, and then cover with a layer of the lamb shoulder mixture. Spread the remaining basic Kibbeh on top.

Be sure to wet your hands in cold water while doing this as it will make the mixture softer and easier to handle. Cut the mixture in squares and press in the sesame seeds. Drizzle the olive oil and the melted butter over the top, and bake in a 400-F over for about 20 minutes.

Then lower the heat to 300-F and bake until golden brown.

This should serve eight souls.

A famous Egyptian who was in Canaan before the time Abraham arrived there was named Sinuhe.

His writings of the land and its fertility and its fruit closely parallel those of the Bible.

In one passage the Bible describes the country as a land of wheat and barley, and vines and fig trees.

Sinuhe describes it as a land of oil, olives, and honey, a land wherein, "Thou shalt eat bread without scarceness."

A very simple bread that our Egyptian tourist might have enjoyed is made throughout the Middle East and also in parts of Asia.

There are as many names for it as there are variations. I call it:

PHARAOH'S BREAD

2 cups yellow cornmeal
3 to 5 cups whole grain whole wheat

1 cup whole millet
1 cup honey
½ cup raisins
½ cup chopped almonds
1¼ cup water
¼ cup sesame seed oil
1 tsp salt

This is a bread that requires stirring not kneading, but be prepared to do quite a bit of hard stirring because the mixture gets very thick and takes a bit of muscle. However, it is guaranteed to be very good for your arm and shoulders, so give it a try!

In a large bowl, mix together the cornmeal, whole wheat and the millet (a small seeded cereal, which can be purchased at organic food stores).

Add the honey, raisins, almonds, water, sesame oil, and the salt and start stirring. Keep at it until you have a consistency that won't fall apart.

Divide the mixture and place each half in a well greased loaf pan and bake at 300-F for 1½ hours.

Remove from the pans, let cool and slice.

Serve with more honey.

"But in the fourth year all the fruit thereof shall be holy to praise the Lord withal" (Leviticus 19:24).

Fruits of all kinds were very popular with the folk of ancient times. Our old Egyptian friend Sinhue, who as a fugitive migrated to the land of Canaan, enjoyed the fruits of the land. When he reached the lands of Ammi-Enchi, chief of the lands of North Palestine, he exclaimed, "He let me select from among his choicest estates. It was a fine place with the name of Jaa. There were figs and vines and more wine than water. Every kind of fruit hung on its trees."

History does not relate what kinds of fruit were grown on Sinhue's estate, but if he happened to have peaches, he might have had them prepared as a dessert.

PEACHES A LA SINHUE

½ dozen fine, large peaches
simple sugar syrup

candied ginger, cut up
Peach ice cream
chopped almonds
ground ginger

If you were the "Chef de Dessert" in Sinhue's household, you would:

Very carefully peel, halve and pit the peaches, and put them in the refrigerator to cool.

When they were ready, you would have made the simple syrup, flavored with the powdered ginger and then immersed them in it, and set them aside to cool.

Place two peach halves on a chilled plate for each guest, and fill the centers with ice cream. Sprinkle the centers lightly with the candied ginger and the chopped almonds. Serve immediately.

"And the fish of the sea, and whatsoever passeth through the paths of the seas" (Psalms 8:8).

There are two kinds of sardines in and around the Holy Land; fresh water which abounds in the inland sea, and salt water which are caught off the coast of the great salt sea, known as the Mediterranean.

There are many varieties of sardines, and they are fished from waters bordering on just about every nation that has an oceanic coastline.

How the ancient tribes of Israel prepared them, I don't really know, but one way I think they might be prepared in modern Palestine follows.

SARDINE SANDWICHES

2 cans sardines, drained
2 hard cooked eggs, chopped
12 pitted olives, finely chopped
1 minced hot green pepper
a dash salt, paprika, and some lemon juice
Miracle whip (Aioli sauce)
slices of small cocktail rye bread

Thoroughly combine all the ingredients and mix well. Let stand in the refrigerator for a few minutes, then spread on the rye slices. These make wonderful tidbits to serve before dinner with wine or cocktails.

"And these are they which are sown on good ground, such as hear the word, and receive it, and bring forth fruit, some thirtyfold, some sixty and some a hundred" (Mark 4:20).

Some of the descendants of the children of Israel are today known as "Sabras," meaning they were native born in the modern state of Israel. The name, "Israel," incidentally, means one who wrestled with God.

"And he said unto him, what is thy name? And he said, Jacob. "Thy name shall be called no more Jacob, but Israel. For as a prince hast thou power with God, and with men, and hast prevailed" (Genesis 32:27-28).

Today, the sons and daughters of Israel are wrestling with nature to bring forth produce, foods, wines, and fruits from the rocky terrain and the barren desert.

Among their products is a fine liqueur named, "Sabra" in their honor. It is used in this dessert recipe to enliven the flavor of fruit.

A SABRA DESSERT

4 fresh tangerines
½ lb seedless fresh grapes
1 pint fresh strawberries
2 tbs sugar
1 cup fresh orange juice
⅓ cup honey
1 tbs lemon juice
2 tbs Sabra
1 tbs crystallized ginger

BEFORE DINNER:

Peel the tangerines and separate into sections. Slice the grapes in halves, lengthwise, and gently mix with the tangerines. Carefully wash the strawberries and hull them. Slice them in half and place them in another bowl and sprinkle them with the two tbs sugar. Chill them.

Meanwhile in a small saucepan, mix together the orange juice, the honey and the lemon juice. Gradually bring to a boil, lower the heat and simmer for about 20 minutes. Take away from the heat, let cool a bit and stir in the

Sabra and the ginger.

Add this mixture to the tangerines grape mixture. Chill. Add the strawberries and their juice just before serving.

Chapter Four

In the Wilderness

One of the great burdens of any command position is making and carrying out orders, and when God told Moses to turn back the people of the Exodus, when they first reached Canaan, he was forced to tell them that they had to return to the Wilderness and wander again for forty more years.

The Reason?

God wanted a new generation to enter the Promised Land, not one filled with dissidents and malcontents. He also wanted Moses to have a fine young army of young healthy folk who could fight and win their battles.

And, of course, food played an important part in this development, for the people had to be kept healthy and growing strong. As I indicated earlier, they found that they had to survive, because there was no turning back. And so they learned to improvise, to raise crops, and increase their herds, and by doing this, build a fine strong nation, that would reach and reside in the Land of Milk and Honey!

LAMB:

Peter Paul Reubens painted a wondrous picture of Christ telling one of his disciples to feed his lambs, and sheep were a precious commodity to the people of Palestine. And they are more a part of Bible lore than any other living animal.

Traditionally, lambs were a very important part of sacrifices. They and their rams and ewes also provided wool for weaving, skins for clothing and shelter; and, of course, meat and milk and cheese.

If you will recall, the shepherds that first sighted the Star of Bethlehem were herding their flocks at the time. Jesus made many references to the gentle qualities of lambs. In the song of Moses in Deuteronomy (chap 32:14), he mentions the milk of sheep, the fat of lambs, and rams of the breed of Bashan.

And when the Lord GOD ordered The Passover, he decreed that a lamb should be sacrificed and eaten with unleavened bread. To this day sheep are considered one of the most important food sources in the world. They are herded by the Basques in the Pyrenes, on the great plains of western America, and in the Land of the Prophets of Islam.

I believe you'll find lamb one of the most delectable of all meats. And almost all of it is available to any Biblical gourmet. Heart, liver, brisquet, and shanks are all great eating.

Cherish the lamb for it is rich in lore and was indeed chosen by the Lord.

"Butter of kine, and milk of sheep, with fat of lambs, and rams of the breed of Bashan, and goats, with the fat of kidneys of wheat; and thou didst drink the pure blood of the grape" (Deuteronomy 32:14).

A way to preserve meat, which has been used since early times, is to marinate it, which not only preserves it, but flavors it as well. The Nomads of the desert as well as the Biblical folk learned this long ago, and often marinated strips of meat were put out into the sun to dry, and become a form of what we call, "Jerky." However, one way to take advantage of freshly marinated lamb is to prepare it in the following manner.

MARINATED LAMB STEAKS

2 lamb leg steaks, about 1-inch thick
3 tbs EACH of olive oil and wine vinegar
½ tsp salt
1 onion chopped
fresh parsley chopped
1 tsp fresh rosemary, crushed
butter

TRY THIS FOR A QUICK AND TASTY DINNER:
Put the meat in a flat glass dish, and mix together all the other ingredients, except the butter. Pour the mixture over the lamb and let marinate several hours.

Saute the lamb steaks quickly on both sides in the butter in a skillet. Heat the marinade in a saucepan and pour over the steaks before serving. Garnish with some sprigs of fresh mint, before serving.

"And in the candlestick shall be four bowls, made like unto almonds, with their knots and their flowers" (Exodus 25:34).

Many of the people of the Holy Lands revered the almond. The olden time Phrygians believed it to be the father of all life, since it was the first of the year to bloom. It was a sign of fertility to the Greeks, and the Moslems regarded it as a sign of heavenly hope. And even today the finest almonds in the world come from the Holy Land and are known as Jordan Almonds.

It's formal genus is "Prunus" and it is believed to be closely related to the peach. In any event, Solomon used its likeness in the decoration of his great temple, and its fruit on his famed gourmet table. The sweet almond combines with a myriad of dishes running all the way from rice to chicken, and here might be one way you might like to please your guests with:

AN ALMOND JORDAN CHICKEN

2 fryer chickens, cut up
1 cube butter
2 cups white wine
2 cups water
1 tbs salt
White pepper
2 tbs butter
2 tbs flour
1 cup chopped almonds
½ cup cream
1 tsp paprika

TO BLANCH THE ALMONDS:
Place them in a small saucepan covered with water and bring to a boil. Let cool until ready to handle and slip off the skins. Slice the almonds quite thin.

Wash and dry the chicken pieces; salt and pepper them, and brown them very lightly in the butter. Do this very carefully so it does not get too brown.

Put the chicken in a large dutch oven along with the wine and the water; cover and simmer gently until the chicken is fork tender.

Remove the chicken from the kettle and reserve. Pour off all but two cups of the juices remaining in the kettle. Add the flour to the juices, along with the almonds and mix thoroughly. Let heat until it is thickened, stirring from time to time. Add the cream and continue heating, but DO NOT let it come to a boil! Place the chicken pieces on a serving platter and pour over the sauce and sprinkle with the paprika.

"There is nothing better for a man than he should eat and drink, and that he should make his soul enjoy good in his labor" (Ecclesiastes 2:24).

I can't think of anyone that wouldn't agree with the sentiment expressed in this verse from the Bible. It specifically rewards man the fruits of his labor, and indicates that after a hard day's toil, he and his family should sit down to a well prepared dinner and enjoy every tender morsel. A morsel I particularly enjoy is made from a bird that is not very well known to the Holy Land, if at all, but I'll wager it would have been a center of attraction in any feast celebrating a holy day.

A FRUITED CORNISH GAME HEN

1 (7-oz) pkg herb seasoned bread stuffing
½ tsp allspice
1 cup corasley chopped dried figs, dates, and apricots
½ cup orange juice
½ cup melted butter
grated peel of one orange
4 cornish game hens
½ lemon
Salt

Thoroughly mix altogether the dry stuffing, allspice, dried fruit, orange juice, butter and orange peel.

Rub the birds inside and out with the lemon, and sprinkle with salt. Stuff the birds lightly. Sew or skewer the opening shut. Place on a rack in a shallow baking pan, or grill on your barbecue over hot coals. Watch them and don't get them too close else they will char.

Roast them for 1 hour at 400-F and baste frequently.

If barbecuing, grill the hens 45 minutes to 1 hour, basting very often and turning frequently. Remember to use medium coals and don't get them too close!

Try a five bean cold salad with this, and a good California Reisling, nicely iced beforehand.

"Even the country which the Lord smote before the congregation of Israel, is a land for cattle, and thy servants have cattle" (Numbers 32:4).

A most nutritious variable garnered from beef is ground meat. It can be prepared in countless ways, from the ever popular hamburger to a "Side," a form of steak garnished with beans and tomatoes.

The chances that the Israelis had a portable meat grinder are pretty slim, but they did know how to very finely chop meat and form it into patties and loaves, as well as meat balls.

A way to prepare the latter which is very popular in Israel these days has been adapted for you and your family.

JOSEPHUS MEAT BALLS

½ lb lean ground beef
½ lb lean ground veal
1 egg, lightly beaten
1 clove garlic, mashed
1 onion, chopped
¼ cup oil
¼ cup minced parsley
Salt & Pepper
1 cup bread crumbs
ice water
4 tbs honey
3 tbs lemon juice
2 cups beef consumme

WASH YOUR HANDS AND:
In a bowl, put together the ground beef, veal and egg, and mix thoroughly.

In a skillet, gently saute the onions and garlic, in the oil, until they are soft. Add them to the meat mixture. Sprinkle with salt and pepper and the chopped parsley and add the honey and mix well.

Add the bread crumbs; then mix again, and then after rinsing your hands in very cold water, form the meat mixture into small balls.

Heat the rest of the fat, and carefully brown the balls all over. Add the lemon juice and beef consumme and slowly simmer for 15 to 20 minutes. Serve with some form of cracked wheat, such as Kasha or Bhulgar.

"And I will send grass in thy fields for thy cattle, that thou mayest eat and be full" (Deuteronomy 11:15).

It should be pretty apparent that, like the armies of Napoleon, the travelers in the wilderness traveled on their stomachs, as well. However; instead of living off captured rations, and those provided by the rear echelon, the Bible Children were forced to take their victuals on the hoof, so to speak, and to say the least, their cattle were a major element in their menu planning.

Lacking modern day pots and pans, they used open fires and earthenware utensils. In the process, however, they produced some highly delectable dishes that basically are still with us to this day. One of them is:

A TRAVELERS STEW

NOTE: Use an unglazed earthenware casserole for this, and be sure to soak it well in cold water for ½ hour or so before filling.

2 lbs chuck beef, cut in large chunks
flour
3 tbs butter
3 tbs olive oil
Salt & pepper
1 clove garlic, minced
2 carrots, sliced
1 large leek, (white part) sliced
1 large onion, sliced
3 tomatoes, sliced
1 bay leaf
1 tbs parsley, chopped
2½ cups red wine

1 tbs butter
1 tbs flour
6 onions, quartered
Sliced mushrooms

As you would start any good hearty stew, lightly coat the meat pieces with flour, mixed with salt and pepper, and then brown them in the heated olive oil and butter.

When they are nicely browned, but not burned, transfer the pieces of meat to your earthenware casserole. In the skillet in which the meat has been browned, gently cook the onion, carrots, leek and garlic until soft. Add these items to the casserole along with the spices. Make a mix of the remaining butter and the flour and gradually stir into the casserole. Pour over the wine to cover the meat and vegetable mixture; cover and cook in a 300-F oven for 2 to 2½ hours.

In the interim, lightly brown the quarters of onion and the mushrooms. Add them to the casserole the last half-hour. Serve this with a large bottle of fine red wine and big chunks of garlic bread to sop up the juices.

> *"But your wives, and your little ones, and your cattle, (For I know ye have much cattle), shall abide in your cities, which I have given you" (Deuteronomy 3:19).*

The biblical data for the 40 years covering the "sojourn" in the wilderness is very scanty, but the indications are, as unearthed by the archeologists, that most of that time was spent in the Negeb, quite near the waters of Kadesh. At one time they retraced their steps back to the Gulf of Aqabah, where there were water holes and possibilities for grazing their cattle on its shores.

You can imagine the problems facing the housewife of those days trying to feed her family. Furthermore she had to utilize every morsel of food, as even the leftovers were precious.

A way to show your frugality in a most rewarding preparation is:

HASH FROM KADESH

1 large onion, chopped
6 tbs suet
2 cups diced, boiled potatoes
3 cups ground, or chopped leftover cooked beef

Salt & pepper
¼ tsp oregano
¼ tsp thyme
1 tsp chopped parsley
Mashed potatoes
½ cup heavy cream

Take a fairsized shallow flameproof casserole and in it, gently saute the onions in the melted suet. Now add the diced potatoes and brown well. Turn in the chopped beef, and season with salt and pepper. Add the cream and press the mixture down to slightly moisten it.

Add the spices and parsley and mix well, and press again.

Now cover the top of the casserole with the mashed potatoes, and place in a 350-F oven for 25 to 30 minutes until the potato topping is nicely browned.

> *"And the cook took up the shoulder and that which was upon it and set it before Saul" (I Samuel 9:24).*

One can well imagine the travails of a cook on the trail leading to the Land of Canaan. Under almost primitive conditions, they were faced with the eternal problem of every housewife; coming up with something appetizing for the main meal of the day.

And something that was within the family budget.

Cattle provided many means of sustenance to the Israelites. Hides for clothing and shelter, fat for cooking, and of course, many kinds of food. A wonderful characteristic of beef is that it combines well with all kinds of vegetables, fruits, herbs and spices, and just about everything.

For an economy-size meal, try these ribs. I believe they will become a regular in your home.

BRAISED SHORT RIBS

3 lbs beef short ribs
prepared mustard
Flour
2 tbs oil
1 tsp salt
1/8 tsp pepper

1 (10-oz) can cream of mushroom soup
¼ cup water
1 lemon, sliced
1 tsp Worcestershire sauce
2 medium onions, chopped
3 tbs flour
water
6 or 8 small white cooking onions

Wash and dry the ribs. Spread the mustard on the meat sides. Then roll them in flour, mixed with salt and pepper, and brown in the oil. Pour away the drippings.

Add the mushroom soup, water, lemon slices, Worcestershire sauce, and the chopped onions. Cover and cook over a low heat for about 2 hours, until tender.

Remove the meat from the kettle, spoon off the fat, and then measure the liquid. If needed, add enough water to come to 1½ cups. Return the liquid to the kettle, blend the water and the flour to make a thin paste, and stir into the liquid in the kettle. Stir over moderate heat until the gravy is smooth and thickened.

> *"Now the children of Reuben and the Children of Gad had a very great multitude of cattle: and when they saw the Land of Jazer, and the Land of Gilead, that, behold, the place was a place for cattle"* (Numbers 32:1).

Down through history, mankind has sought tender meat, whether it be beef, venison, or lamb. Many methods have been used to tenderize meat, running all the way from special tenderizing salts to pounding, and to the method used by the Tartars of Ghengis Khan, who placed their meat cuts under their saddles, so that the weight of the horseman, and the motion of their steeds would break down the fibers. Of course, most everyone knows of the Tartar way of cooking beef by impaling it in pieces on swords and roasting it over an open fire.

It has been recorded that the wandering Tribes of Israel, used much the same process, utilizing green sticks of wood, instead of swords.

Personally, I like to use modern day skewers and my backyard barbecue to prepare lovely tender pieces of marinated beef along with onions, peppers, mushrooms, and a good healthy red wine basting sauce.

A WILDERNESS BARBECUE

2 to 3 lbs sirloin steak cut in 1½-inch pieces
1 large onion, minced
1 tsp salt
½ tsp freshly ground black pepper
1½ cups red wine
½ tsp thyme
½ tsp rosemary
cherry tomatoes
small white coking onions
2-inch square pieces of sweet green and red peppers
whole button mushrooms

Stir up a basting sauce by combining the onions, salt and pepper, the red wine, thyme and rosemary and mixing well. Immerse therein the pieces of sirloin and let them soak up the flavors for 3 or 4 hours.

Now fire up your backyard barbecue pit and let the coals come to a fine light grey ash. Spear the pieces of meat on a long skewer, alternating with the cherry tomatoes, onions, pepper pieces and the mushrooms. Keep a close eye on things, and turn the skewers often to insure evenness of cooking, and make certain you baste often!

When done, remove from the fire; slide portions of the skewer contents onto heaps of rice cooked in a chicken broth instead of water.

> *"And it came to pass, that on the morrow, Moses went into the Tabernacle of witness: and behold, the rod of Aaron was budded, and brought forth buds, and bloomed blossoms, and yielded almonds" (Numbers 17:18).*

I can remember when I was trying to start a budding career as an actor in the community playhouse in Saratoga, California, when, enroute to the theater, I would pass mile after mile of almond groves in full bloom.

The sight was incredibly lovely, and one that most assuredly gave you a grand idea of the blessings of the Lord.

Almonds have a myriad of uses; in cakes, candy, meat dishes, desserts and breads.

This bread is almost a dessert, but it is a basic bread. It is delicious, and interestingly enough it is traditionally baked in layers, which makes it somewhat unique.

AN ALMOND ORANGE BREAD

2 cups all-purpose flour
¼ tsp salt
6 eggs
1 cup honey
1 cup chopped almonds
1 cup orange jam
½ cup golden raisins
1 tbs grated orange rind

Mix together the flour and the salt. In another bowl, beat well the eggs and the honey. Add this mixture to the flour and salt, and mix thoroughly. Butter a cake pan, and pour in ¼th of the batter. Sprinkle this with a bit of the chopped almonds and then spread with some of the orange preserve. Repeat to make four layers.

Cover the top layer with the last of the orange preserve, and the remaining chopped almonds, and finally sprinkle over the grated orange peel.

Bake in a 350-F oven for about 45 minutes. Remove and cool. When ready to serve, place on a board and slice about ¼th inch thick. Then put the slices on a cookie sheet and brown very lightly in a 400-F oven.

Serve with lots more orange preserve.

"There dwelt men of Tyre also therein, which brought fish" (Nehemiah 13:16).

Although the men of Tyre brought fish out of the sea, a great majority of the children of Israel found their finned dinners in the mountain streams that fed the Jordan and the other rivers of the Holy Land.

The word "river" as used in the Bible has several meanings, and generally encompasses any water channel, whether it be small or large. Actually, "The River" was commonly used to denote the Euphrates; however many of the smaller streams were also referred to by the same appelation, and all of them housed fish.

The Bible, as I have said, makes no mention, by name, of any specific fish, so perhaps they did not have any trout in Israel. If not, they have my deepest sympathy for I regard Trout as one of God's more lovely gifts.

After you have made your catch, this is the way to prepare it!

A HEAVENLY TROUT

6 whole trout
½ cup milk
1 tsp salt and pepper
6 small pieces bay leaf
1 tsp thyme
1 clove garlic, mashed
12 strips of beef bacon
2 tbs oil
¼ lb. butter
chopped parsley

Season the milk with the salt and pepper, and then dip the trout in it. Mash together the thyme and garlic. Place a piece of bay leaf inside each trout and add a bit of the garlic, thyme mixture.

Now wrap each fish in 2 pieces of the beef bacon and put them in a well buttered baking dish. Sprinkle them with the chopped parsley and as they cook, baste them with their juices and melted butter.

Bake, uncovered at 400-F until the bacon is nice and crisp. Serve them with lemon wedges, if desired, or place them on whole slices of toasted bread, and surround them with mashed potatoes and crisply cooked fresh green beans.

"We remember the fish, which we did eat in Egypt freely, the cucumbers and the melons, and the leeks and the onions, and the garlick" (Numbers 11:5).

Melons, some rough on the outside, some smooth as glass; all of them filled with the softly colored fruit of the vine. Soft and sweet, and ready to be eaten in combination with other fruits and vegetables, or often with meats.

Tomatoes, I admit, did not exist on the plains of the Wilderness, but their addition to these other foods of the Bible makes for a delicious summer salad.

FRUIT OF THE DESERT

1 honeydew or cantelope melon
3 medium firm tomatoes, peeled and seeded
2 fine large cucumbers

Salt
1 tbs chopped fresh parsley
2 tbs chopped fresh mint
2 tsps chopped green onions

To get the most out of this flavorful and colorful salad, you must:
Cut the melon in half and take out the seeds. Cut the meat out of the melon and cut it into cubes. (If you wish to be fancy, you can use a ball cutter). Reserve the shells, and chill them. Peel the cucumbers and cube them the same size as the melon cubes. Sprinkle the cucumber pieces with salt and let stand for about 30 minutes, then rinse and drain them. Make a standard vinegrette dressing and combine the melon, cucumbers, tomatoes, mint and chopped onions, and pour the dressing over all, and chill. Pour portions of the salad into the reserved melons shells and serve with a crusty bread.

> *"Thus saith the Lord, as the new wine is found in the cluster, and one saith, destroy it not; for a blessing is in it" (Isaiah 65:8).*

After the Exodus and prior to the forty years of life in the wilderness, the Children of Israel neared the land of Canaan and Moses sent out scouts to explore it.

> *"And Moses sent them to spy out the Land of Canaan, and said unto them, get you up this way Southward, and go up into the mountain: and see the land what it is; and the people that dwelleth therein, whether they be strong or weak or few or many" (Numbers 13:17-18).*

They returned with a huge cluster of grapes, so large, according to the Scripture, it took two men to carry it. This was when Moses was told that Canaan was a "Land of Milk and Honey." The scouts had undoubtedly entered the "Brook of Eschol," which means the Valley of the Grapes, which lies Southwest of Hebron. An area that to this day is rich in grape vines. Fine bunches of grapes ranging from 10 to 12 pounds are not a rarity.

It seems somewhat axiomatic therefore, that when the long trek was finally ended, and the Israelites finally settled in Palestine, that they would begin cultivation of those fabulous grapes from the Brook of Eschol.

In my correspondence, regarding this book, with the famed Brother Timothy, F.S.C., the Cellarmaster of the Christian Brothers wineries, he told of a book in his possession that tells of excavations at Gideon, and the discovery of parts of wine jugs marked, "Gideon."

> *"Go thy way, eat thy bread with joy, and drink thy wine with a merry heart" (Ecclesiastes 1:1).*

These are the words of Ecclesiastes, the Preacher, the son of David, King in Jerusalem.

Many folk of deep and sincere religious belief, do not countenance the use of wine or alcohol in any form, which, of course is a belief to be respected.

However, aside from the fact that wine is a food, and has nutritive value, it is valuable as a flavoring agent. It might be of interest to those who abhor wine, that all of its alcohol will burn off once the food being cooked reaches a temperature of 75-F, thus imparting only the flavor of the grape to the dish, not the essence of its distillation.

The fact remains that wine has been a part of mankind's life for many centuries. It has enlivened our festivals and weddings, broadened our commerce, and provided a livelihood for millions of people.

So I suggest you raise your glass to the "Brook of Eschol," and enjoy its fruits along with all the other fruits of the earth.

Grapes that grow the best wines flourish in the temperate zones of our earth, mostly North of the Equator. The largest wine producers are France, Germany, the nations surrounding the Mediterranean, and the United States.

Needless to say, a good wine does wonders for fine food. For the gourmet, it helps to clear the palate, aids in digestion and disposition, and provides nutrition. Consumed with intelligence, it can be a means of turning a modest meal into a banquet.

These recipes that follow are intended only to intoxicate your taste buds, not your heads!

> *"Drink no longer water, but use a little wine for thy stomach's sake and thine often infirmities" (I Timothy 5:23).*

The tenderness and taste of young veal can be attested to by anyone who has enjoyed it. I'm not certain, however that the Children of Israel ate much of it, except on ceremonious occasions, as they must have needed their cattle to reach maturity in order to propagate their herds.

If you will recall, however, it was a calf that Abraham prepared for the

Lord, when the Lord and two of his angels appeared before him in the Plains of Mamre.

"And Abraham ran unto the herd, and fetcht a calf tender and good, and gave it to a young man; and he hasted to dress it" (Genesis 18:7).

An easy method of preparing a most tasty dish using veal, is to saute it with several herbs and spices.

WINED HERBED VEAL

2 lbs veal scallops
Butter
1 cup dry white wine
Chopped green onions
½ tsp basil
¼ tsp oregano

Gently pound the veal slices until they are almost paper thin, and then saute them in some butter. Add the onions, and let them cook until they just begin to color, then add the wine and the spices.
Quickly stir in a bit more butter and stir until it is melted. Serve the veal with the sauce poured over.

"But of all clean fowls, ye may eat" (Deuteronomy 14:20).

Of all the clean fowls, the one most prized in today's economy is probably the chicken, and its parts. And one of those prized parts is the liver.
Although the Bible mentions liver in a somewhat perfunctory manner, one can rest assured that chicken livers were a part of the daily fare eaten by the Children of Israel, as they were a very frugal folk.
If you have a chafing dish, you can make a modern day version of an old brazier recipe from times gone by.

WINED CHICKEN LIVERS

½ cup diced bacon
2 tbs green onions, chopped

2 tbs sweet red peppers, chopped
1 lb. chicken livers
flour
¼ tsp thyme
¼ tsp rosemary
½ cup red wine
¼ cup pitted black olives
¼ cup pitted green olives
chopped parsley

Use the top pan of your chafing dish directly over the flame. Saute the bacon along with the onions and the peppers until the bacon is lightly browned. Then lightly coat the chicken livers with flour and add them to the chafing dish.

Cook them for several minutes until they are nicely browned on all sides. Add the spices and the wine and let the mixture cook for 5 to 6 minutes. Add the olives and let them heat through. Serve over English muffins, and garnish with parsley.

> "Now learn a parable of the fig tree; when his branch is yet tender, and puttet forth leaves, ye know that summer is nigh" (Matthew 24:32).

As long ago as 3000 BC figs were used as a sweetner. Not only Egypt, but the early Phoenicians grew them both for garden decoration and for food. At one time in Greek history, the fig was deemed to be sacred, and it was so highly regarded that its use by common people was banned.

Although the fig was not quite as popular in Palestine, as was the date, it was used in a variety of dishes, and along with the date was dried and carried by the roving desert nomad.

Prepared while they are in season, and fresh, they make a most delectable dessert.

SPICY FIGS

Fresh figs
3 tbs powdered sugar
1 tsp cinnamon, ground
1 cup Marsala wine

¼ cup Cognac or Brandy, or a liqueur
cinnamon sticks
cloves

Thoroughly cleanse the figs by washing and remove the stems. Place them in a rather deep dish. Cover to about ½ their thickness with the sugar, ground cinnamon, which has been dissolved in the cognac and wine. Add a few whole cloves and let marinate for 1 hour in the refrigerator. Serve in individual portions, each sprinkled with a bit more sugar and cinnamon, and garnish with short pieces of cinnamon. Serve with ice cream or sherbet.

"And Melchizedek King of Salem brought forth bread and wine" (Genesis 14:18).

Wine afficionados will argue until the dawn about the serving and choice of wine, and whether or not a red wine should only be served with a red meat, and white wine with a white meat and fowl. It seems somewhat improbable that the ancient Romans, Greeks, Arabs, and Hebrews observed such niceties. Wine was something to be enjoyed and used not only to add pleasure to a meal, but to give flavor to otherwise drab dishes.

Try flavoring your sauces and cooking liquids with wine. You will perhaps find a whole new way of heightening the flavor and pleasing the palate. There is a reason for the hundred or more mentions of wine in the Bible. It's presence gave an added joy to the food and to life itself.

A simple white sauce that can be served over innumerable dishes can be greatly enhanced with a touch or two of a white wine or a sherry.

"A JOYOUS WHITE SAUCE"

2 tbs flour
2 tbs butter
1½ cups fish stock
2 tbs light white wine, or dry sherry
½ cup heavy cream

Melt the butter and stir in the flour to make a roux. Slowly add the fish stock, and then the wine, constantly stirring. Finish the sauce off with the cream and serve over fillets of sole, or any other white fleshed fish.

"And if the burnt sacrifice for his offering to the Lord, be of fowls, then he shall bring his offering of turtledoves or of young pigeons" (Leviticus 1:14).

Squabs, like turtle doves and other birds played an important role in the life of the people of Bible times, and they still do today. And if you wish to make an offering to your family tribe, and its leader, you might try this recipe. It's different and quite simple to prepare.

A SAVORY DOVE

4 squabs, or other small birds
Salt and pepper
¾ cup seedless green grapes
½ cup chicken stock
¼ cup white wine, or sherry or madeira
1 tbs lemon juice

Rub the squabs inside and out with salt and pepper. Heat the butter in a skillet; add the squabs and cook slowly until the birds are lightly browned and tender. Add the grapes, wine, and lemon juice. Cook quickly until the liquid is reduced by one third.

Serve squabs on toast slices and spoon sauce over them. They may be garnished with a few sprigs of parsley, if you like.

"From unto above the door were cherubims and palm trees made, and on the wall of the temple" (Ezekiel 41:20).

The date, as a fruit is not specifically mentioned in the Bible, but its creator, the Date Palm is mentioned some 20 odd times. Actually dates are one of the oldest food trees, going back some 5000 years in antiquity. Without them the ancient desert traveler would have perished.

Also the date palm played a large role in religion. An ancient Arabic poem proclaims that the date palm was created from the earth that was left over from the creation of Adam.

With honey and nuts, it makes any number of delicious dishes, including:

A DESERT NUT CAKE

6 eggs
¾ cup sugar
½ cup honey
1½ cups fine bread crumbs
1½ cups chopped almonds
3 cups chopped dates
2 tsps almond extract
Filling
Dates for decoration

THE FILLING

2 cups chopped dates
½ cup sugar
1¼ cups water
½ cup coarsley chopped almonds
1 tsp almond extract
1 tsp vanilla

STUFFED DATES

1 cup finely chopped almonds
¼ cup orange marmelade
2 tbs butter
36 large pitted dates
Powdered sugar

TO MAKE THE CAKE:
    Beat the eggs until they thicken. Slowly add the sugar and honey and continue beating. Now fold in the bread crumbs, almonds, dates, and the almond extract. Divide the batter between two well buttered layer cake pans, and bake at 350-F for about 40 minutes, until the cakes are firm. Remove and cool on racks.
    Spread the filling between the layers and decorate the cake with stuffed dates.

TO MAKE THE FILLING:
Combine the dates, sugar and water, and cook over medium heat until the mixture is thickened. Stir in the almonds, extract and the vanilla. Let cool.

TO STUFF THE DATES:
Combine the nuts, marmelade, and butter. Mash until well blended. Stuff the dates with the mixture, and then roll them in the sugar.

Chapter Five

Canaan

"**M**inea, Hadhraout, Kataban, and Sheba."
Names to conjure with? Most assuredly, for they were the four kingdoms that were known in Solomon's time, as the spice kingdoms.

Solomon had a high regard for spices, as he set a fine table. He not only imported them, but he grew his own Saffron in his beautiful gardens.

Did you know that it takes approximately 225,000 stigma of the Crocus flowers to make a single pound of Saffron? No wonder spices have been, and still are, expensive. Fortunately, a little bit goes a long long way, and if used properly will enhance the flavor and the taste of many foods; meats, fowls, and vegetables all included.

In Bible times, they were, of course, even more expensive. They were carried by caravans all the way across Southern Asia to Yemen, (which was then the land of the Queen of Sheba) and then on camel back up the Arabian peninsula to the edge of the Mediterranean to Tyre and Sidon, where they were transhipped to Rome and Greece.

> *"And they sat down to eat bread; and they lifted up their eyes, and looked and, behold, a company of Ishmeelites came from Gilead with their camels bearing spicery, and balm, and myrrh, going to carry it down to Egypt" (Genesis 37:25).*

You will recall that Myrrh was one of the treasured gifts presented to the Christ Child by the Magi.

It is an aromatic gum resin derived from a species of woody plants. It is largely used in the East in the making of incense and perfumery.

Balm is also a gum resin, which in Bible days was largely produced in Gilead, hence the term, "Balm of Gilead." What ever was in the spicery portion of that caravan can only be a matter of conjecture, but one can assume there were cloves, cinnamon, and assuredly saffron and pepper. Pepper, you know, was so valuable that a small handful would buy a man a wife!

I have five spice racks and a cupboard of spices in my home. Some from China, India, Spain, Mexico, as well as the United States. Not to mention those from Ceylon, The Spice Islands, Borneo, and so on.

I don't recommend that you do the same unless you strongly wish to become a cookbook author! But you should have a small but adequate supply so you can try some of these delectable recipes. (For goodness sake; keep your spices out of direct sun light!)

"And upon the nobles of the children of Israel, he laid not his hand: Also they saw GOD, and did eat and drink" (Exodus 24:11).

The serving of a fine appetizer is a way to titillate the appetite, and their selection should be that which leads to the repast to follow.

AN APPETIZER FROM SHEBA

1 8-oz jar candied ginger, in syrup
3 (8-oz) pkgs cream cheese
1 tbs ginger syrup, from the jar
A dash salt
1 cup cashew nuts, chopped
1 can, or jar, green pears
1 jar red preserved pears

Remove the ginger from the syrup and chop fine.

Beat and spoon the cream cheese until it is soft, smooth, and very creamy. Blend in the finely chopped ginger and the ginger syrup and the salt. You can also add a bit of very finely chopped parsley to give it color, if you desire. Shape the mixture into a log roll, and roll it in the chopped nuts.

Wrap it in waxed paper and refrigerate for several hours. Serve it on a chilled platter, garnished with the preserved colored pears.

"And she gave the King a hundred and twenty talents of gold, and of spices very great store, and precious stones; there came no more such abundance of spices, as these which the Queen of Sheba gave to King Solomon" (I Kings 10:10).

The inhabitants of the Land of Canaan, during Solomon's reign were principally shepherds and tradesmen, who like to stay in one place and ply their trade. It makes sense inasmuch that after forty years of wandering in the wilderness, they wanted to stay put for awhile.

The Arabic folk, however, were people of the desert and enjoyed being constantly on the move, which is why, with their camels, they became the forerunners of the teamsters of today, moving the goods of commerce across the desert from one Bible land to another. And it was their great caravans that brought the spices to the Eastern world, and finally to Spain, France, Rome and Greece.

In the process, they became somewhat experts in the uses of spices for their own gustatory pleasure, and one exceedingly flavorful stew that they still prepare is an:

ARABIC TANGERINE

3 lbs beef stew meat
¼ lb butter, or margarine
1 tsp ginger, grated
1 tsp Tumeric
Salt
1 bunch parsley
1 stick cinnamon
3 minced onions
water
4 tbs honey
Juice of 1 orange
1½ lbs pears, cored and halved, but not peeled
more butter
Sesame seeds

An Arab would cut the meat into small chunks. And then place them in a large kettle with 2 cube of butter, the ginger, tumeric, salt, parsley, cinnamon, one of the onions, and enough water to barely cover. When you have done this; cover the pot and simmer for 1½ hours until the meat is fork tender. (It might even take two or 2½ hours depending upon the quality of the beef).

Cook until the liquid is a thick velvet-like sauce.

Remove the cinnamon stick and add the two remaining onions.

Cook and stir until the onions are tender and well blended in, and then add the honey. Simmer for another 15 minutes. Now add the orange juice, and let stand for a short time.

One half hour before serving, place the pear halves in a skillet with a nice sized piece of butter, and fry them gently until they are very lightly browned. Add them to the stew. Don't over cook them as they will become mush. In another skillet brown some sesame seeds and add them to the stew just before serving.

"Spikenard and Saffron; Calmus and Cinnamon, with all trees of Frankincense" (Song of Solomon 4:14).

Saffron, today as well as in King Solomon's time is and was the most expensive spice in the world. In this day and age it is grown mainly in Spain, but in Solomon's time his main source were his gardens, which abounded in Crocus plants, which produces Saffron. Needless to say, Saffron was a favorite for seasoning the foods served on Solomon's table.

Used in conjunction with a fine chicken, it will guarantee a rare and pleasurable meal.

SOLOMON'S SAFFRON CHICKEN

2 (2-lb) frying chickens cut up
Salt and pepper
½ cup olive oil
2 cups minced onions
1 tbs chopped parsley
1 cup flour
1 cup dry white wine
2 cups water
¼ cup sliced almonds
2 hard boiled egg yolks
1 tbs minced parsley
1/8 tsp crushed Saffron threads

As always, wash the chicken and then dry it. Sprinkle it lightly with salt and pepper; dip the pieces in flour and shake them to take away the excess. Heat the olive oil in a large heavy frying pan, and when it is sufficiently hot add the chicken, a piece at a time, starting with the dark meat. Follow with the white meat pieces and brown all of them to a lovely golden color. Now put them in a casserole.

Save 2 tbs cooking fat from the skillet, and discard the rest. Add the onions and cook them until they are tender, but not browned.

Spread the onions over the chicken in the casserole, and add the parsley and the wine and water and bring to a boil. Reduce the heat; cover and simmer for 30 minutes. Make a paste, using the back of a spoon, out of the egg yolks, garlic, and saffron. Thin it with a little of the casserole liquid and then gradually stir it into the casserole.

Recover and cook for about 5 minutes longer.

Take out the chicken pieces and put them on a heated platter to keep warm.

Turn up the flame under the casserole and bring the mixture to a boil and cook it until it is reduced by half.

Taste for seasoning and pour over the chicken pieces. Serve at once.

> *"Give us this day, our daily bread" (Matthew 6:14).*
> *"For every beast of the forest is mine, and the cattle upon a thousand hills" (Psalms 50:10).*

It has been said that the enclosure of beef in dough was first created in England to honor the Duke of Wellington, following his defeat of Napoleon at Waterloo.

However, I can well remember, as a young lad, eating some of the most delicious meals I have ever had, prepared by a Lebanese family that lived in our neighborhood. One of those dishes was a boneless chuck roast, wrapped in a Near East bread dough, after it had been slowly simmered with spices and vegetables, and then removed from the kettle and wrapped in the dough, and placed in the oven, where the dough crisped and at the same time absorbed much of those delicious meat and vegetable juices.

Such a dish was certainly not named for a British Duke, and it's certain that its origins went back to the earliest times of the Mediterranean. It is entirely possible some variation was served to Solomon's guests. Whatever, here is a Near Eastern way to prepare a roast of beef. I call it:

"KING SOLOMON'S ROAST"

1 (5-lb) boneless chuck roast
Salt & pepper
sliced carrots, celery, onion, parsley, bay leaf
½ tsp thyme
½ tsp rosemary
2 pkgs dry yeast
½ cup honey
8 cups all-purpose flour
1½ tsps salt
¼ cup olive oil
½ cup sesame seeds

Have your butcher roll and tie the beef, and trim it of fat. Smear the meat with butter or margarine, and place it in a flat pan on a bed composed of the sliced carrots, celery, onion and parsley, and the bay leaf. Mix together the thyme, rosemary, salt and pepper and sprinkle it over the roast, covering all sides. Roast in a 350-F oven for 12 to 15 minutes per pound. When it is done to your liking, remove it from the oven and let cool slightly.

In the meantime, put about ¼ cup lukewarm water in a bowl, and sprinkle in the yeast. Stir it well to thoroughly dissolve the yeast, and then cover the bowl and set it in a warm, draft free place and let it rest for 5 to 6 minutes.

Take a bigger bowl and combine the flour and the salt. Poke a well hole in the center with your fingers, and pour in the yeast, honey, olive oil, and the remaining 2 cups of lukewarm water. Mix slowly, gradually stirring in the flour until a workable dough is formed.

Add more water, a bit at a time, if needed. Work the dough into a ball and knead it until it is smooth and elastic.

Place it in a bowl, cover with a towel and set it in a warm place to rise. When it is about double in size, punch it down, separate it into two pieces and let it sit and rise for another 30 minutes.

On a large floured surface roll out the dough into two large pieces about ¼-inch in thickness.

When the meat is cool enough to handle, place it on one piece of the pastry, and then cover it with the other piece and pull them together, including the ends to completely enclose the meat. Seal the edges with water, and use any left over dough to make decorations. Place on a flat baking pan, brush with some beaten egg yolk and bake at 450-F for 20 minutes, until the crust is nicely browned. Serve sliced and enjoy!

TANGERINE GLAZED CORNISH GAME HENS

4 rock cornish game hens, about 1 lb each
4 tangerines, peeled, segmented & seeded
12 whole pitted apricots
oil
Salt
Saucy tangerine glaze
cooked rice

Thaw hens, if frozen, and pat dry with paper towels. Fill cavities with tangerine sections and apricots. Close securely with skewers. Brush generously with oil or butter. Sprinkle on all sides with salt. Place in shallow baking pan and bake at 350-F for 1½ hours. During the last 30 minutes of roasting, baste several times with saucy tangerine sauce. Place hens on hot rice, and serve with remaining glaze. (Makes 4 servings)

SAUCY TANGERINE GLAZE

2 tbs cornstarch
2½ cups water
3 tbs honey
8 pitted apricots, snipped into quarters
2 tsps grated tangerine peel
2 tangerines, peeled, segmented and seeded
¼ tsp salt
2 tbs lemon juice

Place cornstarch, water, honey, apricots and tangerine peel in a medium saucepan. Stir one or twice and let stand 15 minutes. Bring to a boil over medium heat, stirring constantly. Boil 1 minute and remove from heat. Cut tangerine segments into halves or thirds and stir into sauce, along with salt and lemon juice.

"DURO WAT"

"And he will appoint him captains over thousands, and captains over fifties; and will set them to ear his ground, and to reap his harvest, and to make his instruments of war, and instruments of

his chariots.

And he will take your daughters to be confectionaries, and to be cooks and to be bakers" (I Samuel 8:12 and 13).

Without a question, the mightiest King of the Holy Land was Solomon, who ruled almost all of North Arabia even unto the lands of the Golden Crescent, comprising what we know in this day as the countries of Jordan and Iraq, Syria and Lebanon.

But in the generations to follow, there arose in what is now Ethiopia, another mighty King who was called, "Prester John" or John the Presbyter. Actually an Emperor, he was so mighty that more than a hundred kings paid him homage.

He was called "Prester John," because he was the first to introduce Christianity to that part of the world.

A wonderous King; he had no poverty in his lands; he even had a form of free medical care, and he was indeed loved by his people, and feared by his enemies.

He was also renowned for his love of good food, and one of the dishes that has come down through the centuries in Ethiopia is called a "Doro Wat," which is chicken stewed in a hot pepper sauce. It is a most unusual dish, and one that will pleasure your palate just as it did that of "Prester John." However, I must warn you this takes most of a day to prepare!

Two major ingredients of this exotic dish must be prepared in advance so I suggest you prepare these basics first.

NITER KEBBEH

2 lbs sweet butter, cut into small pieces
1 onion, peeled and coarsely chopped
3 tbs chopped garlic
4 tsps chopped ginger root
1½ tsps tumeric
1 cardomon pod, crushed
1 piece, stick cinnamon
1 whole clove
1/8 tsp ground nutmeg
Cheese cloth

In a large saucepan, heat the butter gently, but do not let it brown. Slowly increase the heat and bring the butter to a boil. When the top of the butter is nice and foamy, stir in the finely chopped garlic, the ginger (an easy way to chop this is to freeze it first), tumeric, cardomon, cinnamon, clove and nutmeg. Reduce the heat and simmer uncovered and undisturbed for 45 minutes, until the milk solids on the bottom of the pan are golden brown and the top is clear. Very slowly pour the clear liquid into a bowl, straining it through at least several thicknesses of cheesecloth, that are dampened. Discard the seasonings. If, by chance you have any solids in the strained liquid, strain it again, else it will become rancid. Put it in a jar, seal tightly and keep in the refrigerator until you start the "Doro Wat."

BERBERE

1 tsp ground pepper
½ tsp ground cardomon
½ tsp ground coriander
½ tsp fenugreek seeds
¼ tsp ground nutmeg fresh grated
¼ tsp ground cloves
1/8 tsp ground cinnamon
1/8 tsp ground allspice
2 tbs finely chopped onion
1 tbs finely chopped garlic
2 tbs salt
3 tbs dry red wine
2 cups paprika
2 tbs ground hot red pepper
½ tsp fresh ground black pepper
1½ cups water
2 tbs vegetable oil

In a heavy large saucepan, gently toast the spices, including the allspice over very low heat for about 2 minutes, stirring them, until they are heated through. Remove from the fire and let cool for a few minutes.

Put together the toasted spices, onions, garlic, 1 tablespoon of the salt and the wine in a blender and mix until it is a smooth paste.

Combine the paprika, red peppers, black pepper and the rest of the salt in a saucepan and again cook them over a very low heat until they are heated, shaking the pan so they don't char. Then stir in the water, a little at a time, and then add the wine-spice mixture. Stir with a will, and let cook over very low heat for 10 to 15 minutes. Be very careful this does not burn!

Transfer the mixture to a jar, and pack tightly. Let it cool at room temperature, then cover it with enough oil to make a film ¼ inch thick. Cover and refrigerate until ready to use.

Both the Berbere and the Niter Kebbeh will keep in the refrigerator for from 2 to 3 months.

DORO WAT CHICKEN

1 3lb chicken, cut into small pieces
2 tbs fresh lemon juice
2 tsps salt
2 cups fine minced onions
¼ cup "Niter Kebbeh"
1 tbs fine minced garlic
1 tbs fine minced ginger
Fresh ground black pepper
¼ tsp fenugreek seeds crushed
1 tsp ground cardomon
1/8 tsp ground nutmeg
¼ cup "Berbere"
2 tbs paprika
¼ cup dry wine
¾ cup water
4 hard cooked eggs

Prepare the Niter Kebbeh and the Berbere.
Then wash the chicken, dry thoroughly and rub the pieces with lemon juice. Let the bird rest for a bit to absorb the juice.
Dry cook the onions in a casserole or deep pan, without any oil or butter, until they are soft and dry. Don't burn! Then stir in the Niter Kebbeh, and when it starts to heat up add the garlic, ginger, fenugreek, cardomon and the nutmeg, and stir to mix well. Now add the Berbere and the paprika and stir again over low heat for about 3 minutes.
Pour in the wine and the water and bring to a boil.
Cook until the mixture is slightly thickened.
Dry the chicken pieces again and place in the simmering sauce, turning them until they are well coated.

Lower the heat, cover and cook for 15 minutes.

Now take a fork and pierce each peeled egg several times. Add the eggs to the chicken and the sauce and coat them with the sauce. Cover and cook 15 minutes more until the chicken is tender. Test for doneness with a fork, and then salt and pepper the birds and the sauce to taste.

Transfer the contents of the pot to a large heated serving bowl, or if you prefer to a large flat bamboo tray, covered with foil, and/or a covered napkin. Eat it with your fingers using pieces of Lebanese Peta bread, and with yoghurt, if you so desire.

Eating this will make you a member of the tribe of Haile Selassie, "The Lion of Judea," who claimed to be a direct descendant of "Prester John!"

> *"And Solomon's provision for one day was thirty measures of fine flour, and three score measures of meal. Ten fat oxen, and twenty oxen out of the pastures, and a hundred sheep, besides harts and roebucks, and fallow deer, and fatted fowl"* (I Kings 4:23).

It is obvious that Solomon and his court were mighty trenchermen who not only enjoyed good food, but insisted on lots of it. In this chapter we are only concerned with the "fatted fowl" however, and since the Bible records geese as being plentiful in that area, it is entirely possible that one of the various kinds of fatted fowl that was served at King Solomon's table was a fine roast goose.

A ROYAL GOOSE

3 lbs onions, peeled and quartered
2 (7-oz) pkgs. cubed herb seasoned stuffing
1 to 1½ dried sage leaves, crushed
¼ cup melted butter
1 can chicken broth, undiluted
A 12 to 14 lb goose
1 tbs lemon juice
1 tsp salt
1/8 tsp pepper
Plum sauce

For the stuffing: cook the onions in lightly salted water until tender for about 15 minutes. Drain and chop them. In a large bowl, toss the stuffing mix with the chopped onion, sage, butter and chicken broth until well blended. Preheat the oven to 325-F., and while this is happening, prepare the goose by removing the giblets which you can discard. Then wash it in cold running water, inside and out, then pat dry with paper towels. Rub the cavity with the lemon juice, and with salt and pepper. Spoon the dressing into the body cavities, close and fasten them with small skewers. (You might also lace the small skewers with kitchen twine to insure the cavities stay closed).

Bend the wing tips under the body and tie the ends of the legs together.

Carefully prick the skin with a sharp fork. Do not prick the meat. Place the goose, breast side up on a rack in a roasting pan.

Roast uncovered at 350-F for 2 hours. Remove the goose from the oven and pour off the fat from the pan and throw away. Now return the goose to the oven and roast 2 hours longer. Remove the goose from the oven; pour off all but 2 tbs of the fat, (which you should reserve for the plum sauce) and return the bird to the oven and roast ½ hour longer.

THE PLUM SAUCE

1 can (1 lb-14 oz) purple plums
2 tbs goose fat
1½ tbs flour
1 cup ruby port wine
A dash cinnamon
A dash cayenne pepper

Drain the plums well; remove the pits and discard. Mash the fruit. In the goose fat, heat the flour stirring well until the flour turns a light brown, which will take 2 or 3 minutes. Gradually stir in the port wine, and bring to a boil, stirring constantly. Boil for 1 minute, and keep stirring as the sauce thickens.

Add the plums, cinnamon and cayenne. Simmer 5 minutes longer, stirring occasionally. Keep warm and serve separately.

Place the goose on a grand serving platter, surrounded with dilled new potatoes, and garnished with small red beets, and shredded lettuce, and carve at the table.

I'm positive King Solomon would have liked it; I pray you will too.

If a joyous feast were held today in Israel, it might well include that lovely bird, the chicken.

And the stuffing for it, might well be Kasha, (Buckwheat-Groats). Also there would be dried fruits as well as raisins and wine incorporated into the dressing.

If you are planning a joyous feast in your home, try this way of making:

"JOYOUS CHICKEN"

KASHA STUFFING:
2 cups whole Kasha
2 lightly beaten eggs
1 large onion, chopped
6 tbs chicken fat
4 cups boiling chicken broth
4 tbs soft butter
3 tbs sugar, or honey
water
3 tbs chicken fat
2 onions, minced
3 celery stalks, minced
3 tbs parsley, minced
½ tsp salt

THE CHICKEN:
A (5 to 6 lb) roasting chicken
½ cup dried, pitted prunes
½ cup all together, dried golden raisins and figs
½ tsp salt
¼ tsp pepper
¼ cup Curacao (A liqueur)
Orange juice
2 cups fine hot cooked noodles

This recipe will require some work, so prepare yourself! The first step in this glamorous recipe is to prepare the Kasha stuffing.

Take a heavy skillet and in it, gently brown 2 level cups of Kasha, which is very common throughout Israel, Syria, and Lebanon.

Add the two beaten eggs and stir well until all the grains are separated.

In another skillet, cook the onions until soft, but not overly brown, in the chicken fat. Add them to the Kasha and then add the chicken broth. Stir well; cover and simmer for 30 minutes.

When the Kasha stuffing is cooked, add the salt and pepper, and the soft butter, toss and set aside.

Wash and thoroughly clean the chicken and set aside. (This can be done while the Kasha is cooking).

You can also gently boil the dried fruits in enough water and sugar to cover until they are tender, then set them off to one side. You can also saute the chopped onions, celery, and parsley along with a little salt and pepper, and set them aside.

When everything is ready, mix together the Kasha, the dried fruits, and the onion mixture and stir well.

Add the curacao and mix again.

Now stuff the bird and seal the openings with skewers, and put it on a rack in a roasting pan and into a preheated oven at 450-F for 15 minutes to give the bird some color. Then lower the heat to 350-F and continue to roast for another hour, basting often with orange juice. Any stuffing that is left over should be put in a casserole dish and cooked along with the chicken the last 30 minutes of roasting time. Remove the chicken from the oven, take out all the stuffing and reserve. Pour a little more curacao over the chicken and return it to the oven to keep warm.

Add the hot cooked noodles to the stuffing and mix thoroughly. Place the chicken on a serving platter and surround it with the stuffing and noodles.

If you like, you can garnish the platter with sprigs of fresh parsley or mint, and with small cherry tomatoes. Carve the bird at the table. Give each person some of the stuffing, and a glass of a good California Cabernet Sauvignon, and thank the Lord for his good works!

> *"Behold that which I have seen: It is good and comely for one to eat and drink"* *(Ecclesiastes 5:18).*

There is more to this verse in the Bible that refers to the fact that mankind should eat and drink and enjoy the fruits of their labours, because it is their due.

And so it is, especially when the food is properly prepared and served as attractively as possible.

The people of the Bible Lands were no strangers to good food and it's service. King Solomon was noted for his fine table, and even the animals and fowls that were used for religious sacrifices were meticulously prepared before being placed on the divine altar.

The whole concept of clean and unclean food is based upon cleanliness and Godliness, and even though all religions do not follow the strict Hebrew customs, it remains that good clean food, cooked to its turn, will certainly warrant one's thanks to the LORD.

Any good festive meal should start with an appetizer, to "make one's juices flow." Here's one to savor.

PATE OF DUCK "IN THE GRAND MANNER"

1 5 lb duck, cleaned and boned
½ lb fresh chicken livers
¾ lb boneless veal shoulder
1 lb ground turkey meat
½ lb beef bacon
1 medium onion, sliced
6 sprigs parsley
1½ oz Cognac
1 oz Amontillado Sherry
¼ cup very finely minced green onions
2 eggs, slightly beaten
2 tsps salt
¼ tsp fresh ground black pepper
½ tsp ground cinnamon
¼ tsp ground ginger
1/8 tsp ground aniseed

This is an unusual Pate and one that will draw many Oh's and Ah's from your guests.

Have your butcher bone the duck keeping the skin as intact as possible, especially that of the breast.

Cut the breast meat lengthwise into ½ inch thick strips. Cut the meat from the second joints and the thighs and set aside. Halve the chicken livers and cut out any membrane. Marinate the strips of duck and the livers in a marinade composed of the onion, parsley, cognac, grand marnier, and the sherry. Let the meats sit in the marinade for at least 3 hours.

Put the remaining duck meat, the heart and gizzard, the turkey, veal and beef bacon through a meat grinder, using the finest blade, at least three times. Now strain the marinade into the ground meat, discarding the onion and the parsley. Reserve the chicken livers and the duck strips.

Add the remaining ingredients to the ground meat and mix well.

Lightly butter a loaf pan, and place the duck skin, outside part down in the pan. Spread half the ground meat mixture in the pan. Place the chicken livers in an even row down the center of the pan on top the ground mixture. Carefully place the duck strips alongside the livers.

Add the balance of the ground meats and put down well.

Fold over any duck skin at the top of the pan.

Cover the pan with a double thickness of foil, and place it in another pan, slightly larger, containing 1½ to 2 inch very hot water.

Bake for two hours in a 350-F oven, and then remove from the oven, discard the foil and let the Pate cool for about 1 hour at room temperature.

Pour off the excess fat from the pan.

Remove the pate carefully from the pan and place it skin side up in a shallow baking pan, and bake it in a 375-F oven for another ½ hour until the skin is nicely browned. Cool again to room temperature, and then wrap the loaf in several wrappings of clear plastic wrap, and refrigerate overnight.

When ready to serve, unwrap it; place it on a chilled platter, garnish with sprigs of fresh parsley, and slice with a very very sharp damp knife.

Although Turkey was not known in the Middle East, for it is a native American bird, but like some birds of that area, it is, in a sense, "sacrificed" for our holidays such as Thanksgiving.

Turkey first appeared in Europe when the Spanish conquerers of the Aztecs took some of the birds back to Spain with them in 1519.

However, here in America, the bird became so popular that Benjamin Franklin wanted it to be our national bird rather than the Eagle. He called the turkey a "respectable" bird. Whatever its origins, it is another of the blessings bestowed upon us by the Lord, and to leave it out of this book would be derelict indeed.

Tarshish means a smelting place, and Solomon sent ships to Southern Spain loaded with copper to be smelted, as well as to the western shores of Arabia, whence they returned bearing him peacocks, apes, gold and spices. Had there been turkeys, he might have had at his table

"A TARSHISH TURKEY"

1 turkey (10 to 12 lbs)
Basting sauce:
3 tbs butter
1 tsp dry mustard

5 tsp Worcestershire sauce
3 tsps Tobasco
1 tsp grated onion
1 tsp chopped green onion

¼ tbs thyme
¼ tbs sage
2 tsps salt
1 tsp pepper
½ cup chopped celery leaves
½ cup chopped fresh parsley
12 cups stale bread crumbs
1½ cups chopped nuts

STUFFING
⅔ cup butter
3 med onions, finely chopped

Wash the turkey, (thaw well if frozen) and dry inside and out with paper towels. Set aside.

Make stuffing by mixing all the ingredients, except the crumbs, and cook gently in a skillet for about 5 minutes. Let cool slightly and add the bread crumbs and toss well. Stuff the bird; truss it well and place on a barbecue spit. Balance it and make certain it is firmly attached.

Make the basting sauce by blending all the sauce ingredients and chilling for a half hour.

Anchor the spit in the barbecue motor over nicely greyed coals and roast for 15 to 17 minutes per pound.

Baste from time to time with the sauce.

Serve this with chilled cranberries, a cold salad, and a cool Chablis wine.

> "What is man that thou are mindful of him? And the son of man that thou visitest him? . . . Thou madest him to have dominion over the works of thy hands; thou hast put all things under his feet. . . . The fowl of the air" (Psalms 8:4, 6, 8).

The turkey was not at all a part of the diet regimen accorded to the Children of Israel, but its popularity has taken it from America to Europe, and from there to the Middle East.

I suppose I am making some kind of a pun in naming this dish, but if you were a turkish housewife, you might well prepare some

TURKEY TURKISH THIGHS

2 lbs turkey thighs
½ cup chicken fat
3 large onions, chopped
2 carrots, sliced
1 cup chopped celery
2 cloves garlic, minced
2 cups chicken broth
Kasha

Put the turkey thighs in a large deep Dutch oven and brown them in the chicken fat. Remove the turkey from the fat, and set aside. Add a bit more chicken fat and in it, saute the onions until they are gently browned. Return the turkey to the kettle, add the chicken broth, garlic, carrots, and celery, and let it simmer, covered for about 2 hours, spooning the broth and the vegetables over it from time to time.

In the interim, cook the Kasha according to the directions on the package, adding some chopped fresh mushrooms and green onions, if desired.

Cut the turkey into bite sized pieces, and serve over mounts of Kasha in soup bowls, and spoon over the liquid from the pot.

> *"And he dealt among all the people, even among the whole multitude of Israel, as well to the women as men, to everyone a cake of bread, and a good piece of flesh, and a flagon of wine" (II Samuel 6:19).*

The idea expressed by Omar Khayam, when he said, "A loaf of bread, a jug of wine, and thou," has a companion thought in the Bible phrase expressed above.

For when David gave the people the bread, meat, and wine, he filled their basic desires and rewarded them. The importance being that even in older times, bread, meat, and wine were considered the ultimate in good living. And so it is in our time. A fine dinner encompassing a lovely bit of warm bread, a fine roast or choice fish or game, and a well-chosen wine makes for a fullness and a pleasure that is too seldom equalled.

WINE BRAISED LAMB

3 lbs lamb shoulder steaks, cut in ½ inch dice
3 tbs shortening
Salt & pepper
Flour
½ cup dry white wine
Water
2 tbs butter
small white cooking onions
small button mushrooms
2 tbs flour
½ cup Sherry wine
½ cup heavy cream
Salt & pepper

Cut up the lamb steaks and dredge in a mixture of the flour, salt and pepper. Braise them in a large Dutch oven in the shortening.

Add the wine and an equal amount of water, cover and let simmer for thirty minutes.

In a saucepan, melt the additional butter and gently cook the onions and the mushrooms. Add to the lamb. Clear out the pan in which the mushrooms and onions cooked, with the sherry wine, scraping into the mixture the small brown bits sticking to the pan. Add the cream, and bring to a boil, and let cook easily for about 10 minutes.

Taste for seasoning and add more salt and pepper if desired. Strain the sauce and add it to the Dutch oven. Cover and cook in a 325-F oven for 35 to 45 more minutes.

> *"And with the one lamb a tenth deal of flour mingled with the fourth part of a Hin of beaten oil; and the fourth part of a Hin of wine for a drink offering"* (Exodus 29:40).

One of the first exports from "The Land of Milk and Honey" was wine which was exported to Rome and Greece. As indicated above in the Bible passage, wine was widely used in religious ceremonies, but it was also drunk quite freely, and some of the wine from the land of Canaan might well have given the Greeks the inspiration for stuffed grape leaves, which are called:

"DOLMAS"

1 cup long grain rice
2 tsps salt
1 jar grape leaves, drained
1½ lbs lean ground lamb
⅔ cup minced onion
pine nuts, shelled
½ cup raisins
1 tsp chopped fresh mint
½ cup olive oil
Lemon juice
1/8 tsp cinnamon
Salt and pepper
½ cup white wine

Take a large skillet and gently cook the onion in the olive oil until golden, but not browned. Add the rice and cook it until it is golden pale. Remove the pan from the heat and add the lamb, pine nuts, raisins, chopped mint, salt and pepper to taste and the cinnamon. Mix all this thoroughly. Spread the grape leaves flat. Be certain they have been well washed and drained, and the stems removed. Now place a spoonful of the filling in the center of each leaf.

Roll up into finger shapes, tucking in the ends.

Place the rolls close together in a casserole, and add the wine, and water enough to just cover them and bake in a 350-F oven for 40 to 45 minutes until the rice is tender. Add a bit more water if necessary to keep the Dolmas covered throughout the baking. Drain off any water remaining before serving.

Add the lemon juice and simmer for 10 minutes longer and then serve.
Try a fine cold white wine with this and rejoice!

> "And Mesha, king of Moab was a sheepmaster, and rendered unto the king of Israel a hundred thousand lambs, and a hundred thousand rams, with the wool" (II Kings 3:4).

Can you imagine what a task it would be to prepare and cook 100,000 lambs?

A magnificent way to prepare a portion of one lamb is to roast it with a succulent sauce. This dish, I think would have made David humbly thank the good Lord.

ROAST SADDLE OF LAMB

Before I list the ingredients, let me explain that a saddle of lamb comprises both the loins on each side of the back, and makes a rare and special treat.

A 7 to 8 lb. saddle of lamb, trimmed of most of its fat
Salt
3 lbs new potatoes, peeled

SAUCE
5 tbs butter
2½ tbs flour
¼ tsp salt
Dash fresh ground pepper
1 can beef consumme, undiluted
2 tbs white wine
1 tsp prepared mustard
¼ cup whipping cream
2 tbs capers, drained

You should invide more than a few guests for this feast, for a feast it is! Serve it with elegance and thank the Lord for his blessings. Pre-heat your oven to 350-F. Wipe the lamb saddle with paper towels and then rub in ½ tsp salt. Place the lamb, fat side up in a large shallow roasting pan. Insert a meat thermometer (be sure it does not touch the bone!) and roast, uncovered for 1½ hours.

Now arrange the potatoes around the roast in the roasting pan, turning them once or twice to coat them evenly with the drippings and continue to roast about 1 hour longer until the thermometer registers 160 degrees.

You can also make the caper sauce. Melt the butter in a medium saucepan, then remove from the heat. Stir in the salt and pepper and the flour and stir until smooth. Then add the beef broth gradually, as well as the wine and the mustard.

Return to the heat and slowly bring to a boil stirring constantly. Let boil for 1 minute. Turn off the heat and stir in the cream and the capers. Keep warm over hot water. To serve, place the meat on a heated platter, surrounded with the potatoes. Garnish with watercress or fresh mint and some cooked whole cranberries, if desired. Pass the sauce separately.

"And bring hither the fatted calf, and kill it; and let us eat and be merry" (Luke 15:23).

The fatted calf has long been the symbol of welcome, and it is justly considered so today, because no other meat, except that of a very young lamb can equal it in tenderness and succulence.

In Bible times, it was generally cooked on a spit turning over glowing coals. On the hearth would be a flat bread baking to a turn, and quite possibly an earthenware pot filled with vegetables.

Such a meal today can be equally satisfying for every member of your family.

A SKEWERED VEAL DISH FROM MOAB

2 lbs veal steak, cubed
¼ cup salad oil
¼ cup lemon juice
¼ cup white wine
Rice

This is a simple dish, yet one that is flavorful. Cut the veal in ¾ inch cubes and marinate them in a mixture of the salad oil, lemon juice, and white wine for several hours.

Skewer the meat pieces and broil under a relatively high heat until it is lightly browned on all sides. Serve over rice or a rice Pilaf.

"And she came to Jerusalem with a very great train, with camels that bare spices and very much gold, and precious stones; and when she was come to Solomon, she communed with him of all that was in her heart" (I Kings 10:2).

Fruits, nuts and spices of all kinds were available in King Solomon's time, due partly to the caravans that came from the land of the Queen of Sheba, and partly because of the fertile land by the shores of the Mediterranean. Spices were very expensive. So much so that a handful of peppercorns would purchase a wife!

One way that several spices, combined with the fruit of the orange tree can be combined to make this lamb dish something that the angels would savor!

ORANGE STUFFED LOIN OF LAMB

A 3½ lb loin of lamb, boned
2 tbs butter
2 tbs onion, chopped
1 cup fresh white bread crumbs
1 tbs fresh parsley chopped
1 tsp fresh grated orange rind
1 tsp green onions, chopped
1/8 tsp thyme
1/8 tsp majoram
1/8 tsp salt
1/8 tsp fresh ground black pepper
2 tbs orange juice
1 large egg, beaten
2 tbs orange juice
⅔ cup bread crumbs
1/8 tsp salt

Carefully saute the onions in butter until soft. Then, in a bowl, add the onions to the cup of bread crumbs, the parsley, orange rind, green onions, and seasonings. Mix well, then add 2 tbs orange juice with *one-half* of the beaten egg. Mix again, then pat the mixture on the inside of the flattened loin of lamb. Roll the loin up, jellyroll fashion and tie at intervals with kitchen string. Place in a rack in a shallow roasting pan; brush with the remaining 2 tbs orange juice pre-mixed with the remaining one-half beaten egg, and then sprinkle with the remaining bread crumbs and salt. Roast for 50 minutes at 350-F.

> *"And she gave the king an hundred and twenty talents of gold, of spices a very great store, and precious stones. There came no more such abundance of spices as these which the Queen of Sheba gave to King Solomon. Besides that he had of the merchantmen, and of the traffick of the spice merchants, and of all the kings of Arabia, and the governors of the country" (1 Kings 10:15).*

Trade with the Biblical people really developed under Solomon, who formed a great mercantile partnership with the cities of Tyre and Sidon.

Solomon sent ships far and wide to bring him foods and treasures of all kinds. His temple was inlaid with ivory, his gardens were resplendent with peacocks brought by the ships of Tarshish. Certainly some of his ships crossed the Mediterranean to far off France where they may have brought him back a recipe for

A SALADE MERIB, THE CAPITAL OF SHEBA

There are as many variations on this salad as there are weeks in a year. Try your own skill, but if you need a guide, here are the . . .

5 medium sized potatoes, cooked, peeled & sliced
½ pkg frozen whole green beans
½ cup olive oil
¼ cup red wine vinegar
2 tbs chopped green onions
1 tsp salt (seasoned)
1 head icebox lettuce separated into leaves
1 can chicken tuna, broken into chunks
2 tomatoes, cut into wedges
1 can small sardines, drained
2 hard boiled eggs, shelled & halved
½ cup ripe, pitted olives

Combine the olive oil, vinegar, green onions and seasoned salt in a jar with a close fitting lid, shake well and let stand. Cook the green beans until just crisp and then combine them with the sliced potatoes, and drizzle most of the salad dressing over them. Let this stand in the refrigerator for at least 30 minutes to season.

Line a shallow salad bowl with the crisped lettuce leaves. Layer the sliced potatoes and the beans on top and cover with the tuna pieces. Arrange the tomato pieces around the edge of the plate, and then place the sardine and egg halves around the sides, along with the olives to make an attractive dish. Drizzle whatever dressing remains over all. Serve with a fine crusty bread and a delicious wine!

Legend has it that the Ethiopian Kings descended in an unbroken line from King Solomon and the Queen of Sheba. Along with this idea was the concept that Ethiopians were of Jewish origin, and having accepted Christ, were the true inheritors of the Hebraic promise.

There is also the legend that "Prester John" was the Emperor who established Christianity in Ethiopia.

However, history tells us that it was actually established during the reign of King Aezanas during the fourth century. Undoubtedly the Ethiopians had strong ties with Egypt and the Egyptian Coptic Church and quite probably there is where they learned the fine art of bread making.

Whatever the source, a major food, and the national bread of Ethiopia has been, and is still today a flat fried bread, which is called, "Injera."

"INJERA"

5 tbs all-purpose flour
3 cups liquid pancake mix
¼ tsp baking soda
3½ cups carbonated soda water
1½ cups water

This is a fried bread, a form that is common throughout the whole of the Middle East-African area, as well as Asia.

Put together the flour, pancake mix and baking soda in a large bowl. Whisking constantly, add the soda water in a slow stream and finally the water, a bit at a time. Whisk until the batter is very smooth and thin.

Strain the batter into another bowl, pressing out any lumps. Heat a 9 or 10 inch skillet, without any grease or oil, until the pan is hot enough to set the batter but not brown it.

When properly heated, take the pan off the heat, and pour in ¼ cup of batter, tilting the pan so that the batter spreads evenly. Cover the pan partially, and cook over moderate heat until the cake is moist, and the top is covered with tiny air holes. The bottom should be smooth and shiny. Be certain the cake does not brown.

Using a flat spatula, remove it from the pan and place it on a warm plate. Keep repeating the process until you have used all the batter.

To serve, spread them overlapping on a flat basket or platter, and fold the remainder into quarters which you can stack in the center. Tear off small pieces and use them to scoop up your food, instead of a knife and fork.

Bread played a very important part in everyone's life in times of yore, just as it does today.

In ancient Egypt, slaves were rewarded at the end of a hard day's labor with pieces of bread; and almost all people called a day "good", if it included bread.

An Egyptian fugitive in Northern Palestine at the time of Abraham once wrote this description of the land of Canaan, "It was a fine place with the name of Jaa. There were figs and vines, and more wine than water. I had bread and wine as my daily fare, boiled meat and roast goose."

The following recipe could be called:

JAA WHOLE WHEAT BREAD

1 pkg active dry yeast or 1 yeast cake
1½ cups hot water
2 tbs honey
1 cup whole wheat flour
2 cups all-purpose flour
2 tsps salt
2 tbs oil
4 tbs sesame seeds

In this day of increasing emphasis on healthy foods, this bread is one of the tastiest and most nourishing.

Put the yeast in ½ cup of the hot water, and let it stand for a few minutes. Meanwhile, put all together, the honey, remaining water, salt, oil, and the whole wheat flour in a large bowl. Add the yeast and stir well. Gradually add enough all purpose flour to make a stiff dough.

Now take the dough out of the bowl and place it on a floured surface, and knead it well. Keep at it until it is nice and smooth and has a satiney look. Return the dough to a well buttered bowl; cover with a cloth, and let it stand in a warm, draft free place. Let rise until it is doubled in size. This should take about 1½ hours.

Return it to the floured surface and punch it down. Knead it again for a few minutes and divide it in half. Shape into two loaves and put them into two well buttered loaf pans. Cover again and let rise until doubled in bulk. Sprinkle the tops with whole sesame seed and bake in a 375-F oven for 45 to 50 minutes.

Remove the loaves from the pans and return them to the oven to crisp the bottoms.

Haile Selassie, for more than 50 years, the Emperor of Ethiopia claimed to be a direct descendant of the "King of Kings," who was, of course, Solomon.

Verse after verse in the Bible attests to the great wealth and power that King Solomon wielded, not only in the lands of Northern Arabia and of the "Golden Crescent," but also on the seas, which his navy sailed with the aid of Hiram.

A very old bread recipe that is still used in many lands to celebrate the birth of Christ, is often called, "King's Bread" and I'm sure you will enjoy it on your festival days.

KING'S BREAD

1½ cups milk
¾ cup sugar
½ tsp salt
1½ pkgs activie yeast
6 tbs warm water
1 beaten egg
1 cup raisins
1 cup currants
¼ cup chopped candied peel
¼ tsp cinnamon
¼ tsp nutmeg
5½ cups flour
6 tbs melted butter
1 cup chopped walnuts

First scald the milk and then add the sugar and salt and dissolve. Dissolve the yeast in the warm water, and then add to the milk mixture. Now stir in the egg, raisins, currants, candied peel, walnuts, cinnamon, nutmeg, and 2½ cups of the flour. Beat until smooth. Add the melted butter and the remaining flour. Thoroughly mix and form into a ball.

Place the ball on a floured surface and knead until it is nice and smooth. Put it back into a well buttered bowl, turn it to grease all sides; cover and let rise in a warm place, away from drafts until it has doubled in size.

Take it out and punch it down. Knead it again for a short time and divide it in half and put each half into a well-greased loaf pan. Cover and let rise again until doubled. Bake in a pre-heated oven at 375-F for about 45 minutes. Test them by thumping them with your knuckle. If they are done they will sound hollow.

Serve this to the "King" of your household along with a fine brandy or Cognac and some good coffee!

> *"And King Solomon spoke, Now therefore command thou that they hew me cedar trees out of Lebanon, and my servants shall be with thy servants: and unto thee will I give hire for thy servants according to all that thou shall appoint: for thou knowest that there is not any amongst us that can skill to hew timber like unto the Sidonians" (I Kings 5:6).*

A nation close to Israel, and one rich in food lore, uses Lebanese lentils to make

A LEBANESE "IMJUDARA"

½ cup lentils
3½ cups water
2 tbs olive oil
2 onions, chopped
2 cloves garlic, minced
½ lb fresh mushrooms, sliced
1 cup Bulghur
1/8 tsp oregano
1/8 tsp cayenne pepper
1/8 tsp paprika
Salt
Pepper

Place the lentils in the water in a large kettle. Bring them to a boil, reduce the heat and cover and simmer for 15 minutes. In the meantime saute the onions and the garlic in the oil until just barely brown. Add them to the lentils along with the mushrooms, Bulghar, oregano, cayenne, paprika and salt and pepper to taste. Cover the kettle and simmer for 25 to 30 minutes.

Serve this delectable dish, piping hot, topped with yogurt or sour cream, if you desire.

(Makes 4 main dish servings or 8 side dishes)

"And the manna ceased on the morrow, after they had eaten of the old corn of the land; neither had the children of Israel, manna anymore; but they did eat of the fruit of the Land of Canaan that year" (Joshua 5:12).

This particular legend is not Biblical, but it comes from the same part of the globe, and involves Ali Baba, who used the phrase, "Open Sesame" to get entrance to the cave of the forty thieves. The reason the word "Sesame" was used was based on the fact that sesame seeds pop easily out of their hulls.

Sesame is widely used in the Middle East and has been for many, many years. One way it is used in Israel, Egypt, and Turkey is ground into a paste and then combined with other ingredients to make a dip for crackers, or chips.

A RED SEA TAHINEH

Grind the sesame seeds in a bit of olive oil, using just enough oil to make a smooth paste. Use a mortar and pestle for this.

*1 cup sesame seed paste
2 cloves crushed garlic
½ cup water
1 tsp salt
Juice of 2 lemons
a dash cayenne pepper
a dash cumin*

Combine the sesame seed paste, crushed garlic, water, salt and lemon juice, cayenne, and cumin and beat until creamy. Use as a dressing for "Falafel," an Egyptian appetizer, or as a dip for crispy breads.

"Or speak to the earth, and it shall teach thee; and the fishes of the sea shall declare unto thee" (Job 12:8).

Sometime ago during my research for another book, I attempted to locate the city of Tarshish, from whence came the ships that brought King Solomon his apes, peacocks, gold and spices. All I could learn was that "Tarshish" meant a place where ore was smelted, and that there were several such places. One on the Arabian peninsula, where Solomon's copper was smelted. One or more on the east coast of Africa, and one in Spain on the coast of the Mediterranean. Such a Spanish smelting place might well have sent Solomon's crews back to their homeland with a recipe for

A MEDITERRANEAN PAELLA

4 tbs olive oil
4 to 6 chicken thighs
1 cup rice
2 cups chicken broth
¼ tsp saffron
¼ tsp salt
½ cup chopped onion
½ cup chopped tomatoes
½ cup peas
2 garlic cloves, chopped
1 cup fish, cut in chunks
1 lemon, cut in wedges

Heat the olive oil in a large skillet over medium heat. Add the chicken pieces and cook for a few minutes on each side. Remove the chicken and reserve, then add the rice to the oil in the pan and stir. Add the chicken broth, saffron, and the salt. Cover the pan and let cook for about 5 minutes. Scatter the green peas, chicken and the garlic about the pan, and bring the mixture to a boil. Add the tomatoes, fish pieces, and place in a 350-F oven for 30 minutes.

Remove the pan from the oven and let it stand for 4 or 5 minutes.

Serve 1 or 2 pieces of lemon with each portion of the Paella, and squeeze a bit of the lemon juice over the rice. Served on a large platter, with the rice mounded in the center, this will make a glamorous dish to present at the table. Be sure to have some bread to serve with this as well as a chilled wine.

"Send therefore now, and gather thy cattle" (Exodus 9:19).

Once upon a time, some years ago, I was the secretary to a very important political person in California, and on our trips about the state we would sometimes repair to a ranch near Livermore in Northern California, which was owned by a fine man, named Max Baer, once the heavy weight champion of the world.

I can't say that Max was the most religious man in the world, but I can state with some authority, that his way of preparing a lusciously thick porterhouse steak over a fine glowing pit of hot coals, fully satisfied anyone's gustatory standards.

I have not been able to find a direct reference in the Bible or related works to a porterhouse steak, but you can be reasonably certain that good sized cuts of meat were often grilled over an open fire. Just make certain, when you grill it, that it has been properly trimmed of excess fat, and then give it lots of tender loving care. This will assure you a great main event for a most magnificent dinner.

"A PALESTINE GOURMET DINNER"

1 porterhouse steak, cut about 4 inches thick
2 lbs fresh mushrooms
1 cube butter
Salt and freshly ground black pepper
Chopped parsley
fine minced onions

Let the steak sit at room temperature for an hour or two to make certain it is ready to grill. Salt and pepper it well, and let it stand a few more minutes.

In the interim, gently saute the well-washed and cleaned mushrooms in the butter. (Button-sized are the best). Add the parsley to the mushrooms as they are cooking, along with the minced onions.

Broil the steak to just exactly the right amount of doneness, you desire, and then place it on a platter that has been warmed, surrounded with chilled crisp lettuce leaves and cherry tomatoes. Cover the top of the steak with the mushrooms, and slice the steak according to the preferences of your guests.

Personally I would like some freshly cooked corn on the cob with this, as well as some crisply cooked fresh green beans, and a relish of some kind. I would keep this dish simple, and not cover it with any sauces; just the juices of the steak mingled with that of the mushrooms.

One other juice I would add would be that of a fine Cabernet Sauvignon, and perhaps some garlic French Bread.

"He causeth the grass to grow for the cattle, and herbs for the service of man; that he may bring forth food out of the earth" (Psalms 104:14).

I am seriously indebted to my Lady, my wife Lois for the following recipe. It is one she developed, much as a Biblical housewife did to economically use all the parts of a slaughtered beef. The people of the early occupation of Palestine had a hard life and care and prudence had to be exercised to the fullest extent. One way to take advantage of ground meat, and win the plaudits of your family is:

BIBLICAL MEAT LOAF

1 lb lean ground beef
1 onion, chopped
1 clove garlic, minced
¼ green pepper, chopped
1 pinch poultry seasoning
1 tsp Lawry's seasoned salt
1 egg
1 small can (8-oz) tomato sauce
Pepper to taste

When Lois makes it, she mixes all the ingredients thoroughly, except the tomato sauce. Then she forms it into a loaf shape and places it into a lightly greased bread loaf pan, and bakes the contents for about one hour at 350-F.

Halfway through the baking time, she removes the pan from the oven, pours off the accumulated grease and then tops with the tomato sauce, and returns the loaf to the oven to finish cooking.

This is easy to prepare and along with some potatoes, and a green vegetable will make a fine dinner.

"And the men did so; and took two milch kine, and tied them to the cart, and shut up their calves at home" (I Samuel 6:10).

The Bible student will note that cattle and calves are mentioned again and again in the book of the Lord. They were not only regarded for their food, but also used as symbols of worship, such as the golden calf of Baal.

In any event, cattle and their offspring were carefully protected, herded and bred in order to provide food, shelter, clothing, and sustenance to the people of Israel.

A choice piece of beef well turned with spices and liquid in an earthenware casserole can be a most delicious dish. One that has been enjoyed down through all the centuries is . . .

A WILDERNESS BRAISED BEEF

2 or 3 large pieces of suet
1 (3-lb) eye of the round
1 clove garlic, crushed
1 tsp salt
1 tsp pepper
¼ tsp nutmeg
¼ tsp grated ginger
2 more pieces of suet
1 onion, quartered
2 carrots, sliced
3 green onions, peeled and sliced
2 bay leaves
Fresh parsley
1 tsp Rosemary
2 cups Burgundy wine
2 cup beef stock

Place the thinly sliced pieces of suet in the bottom of the earthenware casserole. Crush together the nutmeg, garlic, salt, pepper, and the ginger. Rub it well into the meat.

Place the seasoned eye of the round on the suet slices, and add the vegetables, parsley, wine, and the beef stock. Now add the bay leaves, parsley and the rosemary. Place the remaining thinly sliced pieces of suet on top of the roast. Cover the casserole with a heavy piece of foil, and then with the lid. Bake at 350-F for about four hours, until the meat is very tender.

Slice and serve with a creamed horseradish sauce.

"And a mixed multitude went up also with them; and flocks and herds, even very much cattle" (Exodus 12:38).

A fine robust beef stew is as revered as much in Palestine as it is in Ireland, Argentina, France, or America, or just about any other country you can name. I'll aver and avow that "Grace" has been said over an offering of stew, more than any other dish in the world. One of the very beneficial assets of stew is that it uses the more economical cuts of beef, and it provided a full, well-rounded meal loaded with nutrition and plenty of vitamins and minerals.

An old and very much loved stew recipe in the Holy Land is:

"ISRAEL CHOLENT"

5 large carrots
5 medium white potatoes
1 3-lb piece boneless beef brisket
1 tsp salt
½ cup dried apricots
½ cup pitted dried prunes
1 cup brown sugar, packed
3 tbs oil
1 small onion, chopped
½ tsp ground ginger
1 clove garlic, crushed
Fresh ground pepper
1 whole stick cinnamon
8 whole cloves
1½ cups red wine

Soak the prunes and apricots in hot water for 30 minutes and then cut into small pieces. Peel the carrots and slice. Peel and quarter the potatoes. In a heavy dutch oven, brown the meat in oil on all sides. Pour off the excess drippings, and add the carrots, potatoes, salt, sugar, pepper, onion, sugar, ginger, garlic, cinnamon, cloves and the wine.

If necessary, add enough water to barely cover everything.

Cover tightly and simmer for one hour. Then add the dried fruits and simmer for another 30 minutes.

Now remove the meat and vegetables to a large baking dish. Pour the juices over, including the brown bits clinging to the pan, and bake for another two hours until the meat is very tender.

> *"Behold the hand of the Lord is upon thy cattle which is in the field" (Exodus 9:3).*

Believe it or not, a most elegant dish is a pot roast, properly prepared and served. Who the first person was to discover that a long slow roasting of a solid chunk of beef, along with some herbs, spices, and perhaps a bit of wine, has been lost to antiquity.

But to the people of the "Promised Land," such a "Pot Roasting" was very common as it utilized the lesser cuts of beef and provided food for several meals.

When the dread Philistines unearthed the secret of smelting iron, they made swords and other impliments of war. But they also made pots and kettles, probably at the insistence of their wives, which resulted in a more varied and nutritional method of cooking.

Pot roasts have been called, "Royal," have been named after people, and were often an important part of the Nomad's diet.

"TENTED POT ROAST"

1 (4-lb) rump roast
4 tbs melted suet
Salt & Pepper
flour
1½ cups beef stock
1½ cups red wine
1 bay leaf
12 small white cooking onions
½ tbs honey
Water
1 tbs minced parsley
½ cup brandy
½ tbs butter
1 tbs flour
2 tbs cream

Mix together the flour, salt, and pepper and brown the roast in a large Dutch Oven. (Preferably cast iron) Add the beef stock, the wine, bay leaf, the onions, honey, and parsley. Add enough water to just cover the roast, cover and cook, either on top of the stove, or in a 350-F oven for 3 to 3½ hours, basting the meat from time to time. Cook until the roast is fork tender.

Remove the meat from the kettle, reserve the onions, and let the meat stand to settle. Meanwhile, melt the butter, add the flour and stir well. Strain the juices from the cooking kettle, and add to the roux. Stir and cook until the liquid is reduced by half. Add the cream and the brandy. Slice the roast and serve with the onions and the gravy.

"Send therefore now, and gather thy cattle, and all that thou hast in the field" (Exodus 9:10).

If you have cooked the "Duro Wat" that is in this book, a dish from Ethiopia, you will have some Berberi and some "Niter Kebbeh" left in your refrigerator.

An easy way to use some of both the spiced preparations along with some beef chunks and an eggplant to make a simple African stew is an

AFRICAN EGGPLANT STEW

2 lbs beef stew meat, cut in small chunks
½ cup cocoanut milk
2 tbs Berberi
1 large eggplant
Salt and pepper
½ cup Niter Kebbeh

Heat and melt the Niter Kebbeh over a low fire. As it starts to melt stir in the Berberi until it is a smooth thick liquid. Stir well, and add the cocoanut milk.

Blend well and then add the beef chunks.

Cover and simmer for four to five hours. Add the peeled and chopped eggplant about ½ hour before serving.

Here again, use "Injera" bread or "Peta Bread" to serve yourself.

(Note: to make an easy cocoanut milk, simply take a package of unsweetened coconut, add milk, and bring almost to a boil. Let stand for a few minutes and then squeeze the liquid out through 3 or 4 thicknesses of cheesecloth or a towel).

"When I call to remembrance, the unfeigned faith that is in thee, which dwelt first in thy grandmother, Lois, and thy mother Eunice; and, I am persuaded that in thee also" (II Timothy 1:5).

This particular recipe, although it has no biblical background, does call to mind a lady of great faith. It is rather a tribute to one whose faith in the author of this book has inspired its inception, and strengthened his resolve.

There is no biblical reference to potatoes, and the conjecture is that they did not reach the Holy Lands until after the Romans invaded the Lands of the Pics and found them growing in Ireland. And forthwith transported them to the lands bordering the Mediterranean.

Suffice it to say, however, that the faith of Lois, coupled with her culinary skills has produced a potatoe salad that any modern Israeli chef would envy!

A FAITHFUL POTATOE SALAD

4 or 5 good-sized russet potatoes
1 large onion, finely diced
4 chopped hard-cooked eggs
2 sliced hard-cooked eggs
Salt & pepper
1 cup Miracle whip
1 rounded tsp prepared mustard
1 clove garlic, pressed
Juice of ½ lemon
Parsley

Boil the potatoes in their skins; let them cook until done, and then cool. Peel and dice. Put together in a large bowl with the chopped onion, chopped hard-cooked eggs, salt and pepper, and gently mix. Make a dressing in another bowl of the Miracle whip, the mustard, garlic, lemon juice, and taste. The taste should be slightly tart. If not, add more lemon juice. Stir the dressing well and pour over the potatoe mixture and toss gently until well coated. Garnish with chopped fresh green parsley and the sliced hard cooked eggs.

Chill.

> *"Moreover they that were nigh them, even unto Issachar and Zebulun and Nephtali, brought bread on asses, and on camels, and on mules, and on oxen, and meat, meal, cakes of figs, and bunches of raisins, and wine, and oil, and oxen, and sheep abundantly: for there was joy in Israel"* (I Chronicles 12:40).

Like many other foods available in the Holy Land, raisins rapidly became a staple of their daily diet. Raisins traveled well, kept their flavor and taste without special treatment and were easily renewed to plumpness with a simple hot water bath.

Raisins, as everyone knows, are dried grapes, but a very interesting transformation takes place as they are dried. The sugar content increases a great deal, giving them a sweeter flavor and enlarging their nutritive capability. For a delightful desert, try these:

FESTIVE RAISINS

1 cup golden, seedless raisins
¼ cup grated orange peel
1 tbs orange juice
3 tbs light brown sugar
4 tbs port wine
Vanilla ice cream

Wash the raisins and put them in a saucepan with water to cover. Bring to a boil and then set aside to stand for 10 to 15 minutes to plump. Drain them and add the orange peel, orange juice, sugar and the port wine. Let them marinate for 1½ to 2 hours. If you desire, just as you serve them, add 2 tbs warm brandy and set aflame. Pour over vanilla ice cream, and serve with cookies.

> *"And they gave him a piece of a cake of figs, and two clusters of raisins: and when he had eaten, his spirit came again to him"* (I Samuel 30:12).

Simple baked cakes were very common long ago, and some of them have withstood the test of time, and have become delicacies. Such is a carrot cake, one which has become a must for natural food lovers, and also, one which is much admired in the Middle East as a fine dessert.

The following is a basic recipe, which you can embellish by using a different liqueur or brandy or cognac, as you prefer.

CARROT CAKE

9 eggs
1½ cups sugar
1½ cups pureed cooked carrots
2½ cups ground almonds
1 tbs grated orange zest
1 tbs orange Curacao liqueur
½ tsp ground cinnamon

Separate the eggs, and beat together the yolks, carrot puree, sugar, almonds, orange zest, cinnamon, and the orange liqueur.

Now beat the egg white until they are good and stiff, and carefully fold them into the carrot mixture.

Thoroughly butter a spring form pan and pour in the cake mixture. Bake in a 350-F oven for 50 minutes. Cook on a cake rack, and then remove from the pan.

The almond was highly revered in ancient times. So much so that King Solomon instructed the builders of his famous temple to create vessels and other vestal items in the shape of almonds, and even to use almond wood in the construction of many of the urns to be used for religious purposes.

The pungency, flavor, and meaty succulence is today well known to cooks throughout the world. Its uses in the culinary arts are almost without number, and it can be termed one of the more lovely blessings of God. As anyone who has seen an almond grove in full bloom can attest.

AN ALMOND DELIGHT

a sponge cake
2 cups chopped dried fruits, (apricots, prunes, citrus fruits, etc.)
2 or 3 tbs powdered sugar
Toasted, slivered almonds
Israeli SABRA liqueur

Slice a sponge cake horizontally in three equal slices. Cover the bottom slice with a sprinkling of the chopped dried fruit, and then sprinkle with the Sabra. Place the next layer on top and repeat the process. Cover with the final top slice and repeat the process again. Place in the refrigerator to chill slightly, and decorate with red and green maraschino cherries. Just before serving, sprinkle with a bit more Sabra, and serve immediately.

> *"More to be desired are they than Gold, yea, than much fine Gold: Sweeter also than honey and the Honeycomb"* (Psalms 19:10).

Whenever and wherever there have been flowers, there have been bees to gather the sweetness of the blossoms and turn it into a nectare fit for the Lord and his disciples.

There are many mentions of honey in the Bible. Probably the most famous being the description of "The Land of Canaan" being a "Land of milk and Honey."

A most lovely way to combine this heavenly gift with the fruit of the almond tree is to make:

AN ALMOND HONEY

Vanilla ice cream
finely chopped dates
Honey
Chopped almonds
½ tsp almond extract

Mix together the ice cream, the finely chopped dates, honey, and the finely chopped almonds. Add the almond extract, mix well and place in the freezer compartment of your refrigerator to freeze.

Serve in sherbet glasses and top with a red or green maraschino cherry.

Chapter Six

The Time of Christ

"And she shall bring forth a son, and thou shalt call his name, Jesus; for he shall save his people from their sins" (Matthew 1:21).

By the time Jesus was born two thousand years ago, Canaan had become a well populated country, trading with the nations around the Mediterranean, as well as with its neighboring countries. Food of all kinds was cultivated, and much of it was exported. Spices, wines, and fruits of all kinds, as well as cattle and sheep were common in almost everyone's diet, as well as the fish of the lakes and seas.

The fine art of food preparation had become more sophisticated. The folk of the Exodus were more or less permanently entrenched and they no longer had to depend on cooking devices that were easily portable. Ovens were built that could perform a number of cooking functions, and iron pots and pans, in addition to clay vessels were available to use in the preparation of daily meals and for festive occasions.

Jesus was very aware of the importance of food, and made his appreciation very apparent many times, as shown by his concern for the feeding of the multitude on the shores of Galilee, as well as his symbolic use of bread and wine at the last supper.

Prior to the time of our Saviour, Solomon had enriched the love of food with his sumptuous table, and as far back as Abraham, the eating of game such as venison was greatly enjoyed. When the people of the Exodus first came upon Canaan and were refused admission, their first thought was to bewail the fruits and foods that they had left behind in Egypt.

So it becomes only logical that when they finally became entrenched in the Promised Land that they should take advantage of its fruits and growing things, not only in Jesus' time, but just as the modern Israelis do today.

"Israel then shall dwell in safety alone: the fountain of Jacob shall be upon a land of corn and wine; also his heavens shall drop down dew" (Deuteronomy 33:28).

Old tablets, pottery, and documents unearthed in Greece and Rome all testify to the honor paid to wine. Interestingly enough, the Greeks, because they were actually quite temperate, mixed water with the wine, and followed the dictates of their motto, "Nothing in Excess." It has not been recorded however, that the Romans were so inclined.

In the beginning, as has been indicated earlier, much of the wine consumed on both sides of the Great Sea came from the Holy Land. In fact, the story goes that the first thing Noah planted following the flood was a grape vine, thus making him the father of those who love the grape!

In addition to an aperitif to unlock your appetite, you might use wine in this appetizer.

A GOLDEN SCIMITAR APPETIZER

2 medium eggplants peeled and cubed
Salt
olive oil
1 cup finely chopped parsley
1 cup finely chopped red onions
⅓ cup fruity white wine
3 cups drained, cooked Italian plum tomatoes
6 to 8 large green olives, pitted and slivered
2 tbs capers
2 tbs anchovy paste
Salt & pepper
2 tbs ground pine nuts

Sprinkle the eggplant cubes with some salt and let them set in a colander to drain for about half an hour, then remove them and let them dry on paper towels. Reserve.

In a large skillet, heat ¼ cup olive oil, and add the onions, and cook gently for just a few minutes. Do not let them brown. Then add the dry eggplant cubes, and continue to gently simmer. Now stir in the wine, the drained and chopped tomatoes, the green olives, capers, anchovy paste, a very little salt, and some freshly ground black pepper. Bring to a boil, and then lower the heat and simmer uncovered for 15 to 20 minutes, stirring often. Add the ground pine nuts and taste for seasoning.

When ready, neatly mound in a serving bowl, top with the chopped parsley and serve with wafers or bits of lightly toasted Peta bread.

> *"These shall ye eat of all that are in the waters; whatsoever hath fins and scales in the waters, in the seas, and in the rivers, them shall ye eat" (Leviticus 11:9).*

The "fishers" of early times in Palestine were well respected, because they provided a food rich in portein, as well as in flavor.

Jesus was very familiar with the fishermen of Galilee, and often walked and talked, with them, and even sailed with them. And he helped them with their catches, as attested to when he asked them to lower their nets a second time, which produced the great draught of fishes.

One species of fish, well equipped with fins and scales is the lowly sardine, and a fish that is equally fished from the salt sea as well as in inland fresh waters.

This appetizer may well make you a fan of this small fish of Biblical history.

A "LITTLE" APPETIZER

8 canned sardines
4 medium potatoes
1 onion, thinly sliced
6 tbs butter
1 cup heavy cream
Salt

Mash the sardines, bones and all thoroughly in a bowl. Peel the potatoes and cut them in strips a bit larger than matchsticks. (Old fashioned kitchen type)

Grease a casserole lightly, and in it make a layer of potatoes, then of onions, then the sardines, and top with the remainder of the potatoes. Dot with butter and pour the cream over all. Cover and bake at 475-F for about 30 minutes.

Now uncover the casserole, lower the heat to about 350-F and bake until the dish is golden brown and the potatoes are done.

"And there came a man from Baalshalisha, and brought the man of God, bread of the first fruits, twenty loaves of barley, and full ears of corn, in the husk thereof. And he said, give unto the people that they may eat" (II Kings 4:42).

A relatively simple, but very tasty pre-dinner morsel, and one that can be used as part of a buffet, or for an accompaniment to liquid refreshments, and uses items that can be purchased at almost any supermarket.

A HOT ONION RYE APPETIZER

A quick and easy way to make a small, but tasty appetizer, is to mix together the butter, (softened) and the onion mix.

½ cup butter of margarine
1 package onion mix
1 loaf, small cocktail rye bread

Place the bread on a large piece of foil, and spread the slices with the onion butter. Press the loaf together into its original shape, and wrap tightly in the foil.

Heat for about 20 minutes in a 400-F oven, or even over a charcoal fire, turning from time to time so it heats evenly.

"And carry these ten cheeses unto the Captain of their thousand, and look how thy brethren fare, and take their pledge" (I Samuel 17:18).

Legend has it that the first cheese came from the wilderness, when a nomad put some milk into a pouch made of a sheep's stomach, and tied it to his camel, and when lunchtime came, found that the motion of the camel along with the lining of the sheep's stomach had developed cheese.

In this day and age, of course, the making of cheese is a highly developed art. And there are as many cheeses as there are countries on the earth. Each nationality and province has produced its own variety, dependent upon the milk producing animals native to the area, the climate, and the likes and dislikes of the inhabitants.

Most cheeses require a rather rigid temperature control, just as a fine wine does. In fact, there are many similarities in the making and ageing of cheese and wines. And experts in cheese manufacture, WATCH OVER their maturing charges with lots of tender loving care, just as a wine cellarmaster does.

Some cheeses are relatively odiferous such as the famed limburger, which brings to mind a rather famous tale dating from World War II of the young medical officer who was with the invasion until in the South of France he came upon a warehouse containing quantities of Camembert cheese, which was then in the process of ageing and ripening, and gave off a rather strong odor. He ignorantly assumed that the contents of the building were unhealthy and ordered its immediate destruction by fire. And since he did not speak French, no amount of protestation by the villagers could dissuade him. It has been told that a large sum of reparation has since been paid by the American Government to the people of that village.

To the shepherd who watched over his flocks, the lonely rider on the range, the Epicure, such as Brillat-Savarin, who once remarked, "A dessert without cheese is a beautiful woman with only one eye," Cheese has indeed been a staff of life.

You will do well to include it in your daily menu, because it is one of the Lord's natural foods, created to give you health and to help you have a good life! Involve yourself in some of the following recipes, and participate in the world of gustary pleasure.

The good Lord made mankind the recipient of all of the fruits of the earth, and since cattle were presented to Adam in the Garden of Eden, it follows that the fruits of cattle, such as milk and cheese can also be called gifts of God.

There are a multitude of cheeses, some of them long-lasting, some of them pungent, some of them strong, and some mild and tender. As with wine, hearken to your own pleasure and palate and enjoy!

Here follows a brief glossary of cheeses, which you can use as a buying and cooking guide. I would suggest that if you are a true "Tyrophile," you become a member of the Cheeselovers International, in New York State, who specialize in natural cheese, without any additives. I'm certain Mr. Gerard Paul will be most happy to advise you on the uses of fine cheese.

BEL PAESE

A semi-soft cow-milk cheese with a smooth waxy body. From Italy, it can be identified by a light grey rind, and a creamy yellow interior. It is great with desserts, accompanied with a light wine and sometimes fruit.

BLEU CHEESE

A semi-soft blue-mold cow-milk cheese, pasty, sometimes crumbly. It is white, marbled with a blue-green mold, and comes in small and large wheels. Use it for snacks, appetizers, salad dressings, dips, sometimes in cooking, and for dessert.

CAMEMBERT

A soft-ripened white-mold cow milk cheese. Comes in an 8-oz wheel, with a white edible crust, and a soft yellow body. It is wonderful with desserts, with wine, fruits, and with crusty French bread. Serves as a fine appetizer with unsalted crackers.

CHEDDAR

A cheese from England! This cheese is firm to hard, and is made from cow's milk, and has a smooth firm texture. It can be white, yellow or orange, and comes with or without rinds, and in many shapes. Place it on the table, or serve it as a dessert; or use it to make a tasty welsh rarebit. Try it for snacks along with a good wine, a foamy glass of beer, or with some fresh apple slices.

CREAM CHEESE

A soft smooth, buttery unripened cow-milk cheese. Use it as a spread, in making various Hors D'oeuvres, and in making salad dressings.

EDAM

Blessed be the Dutch for they have given us this excellent cheese. Another cow-milk cheese, that is semi-soft and has irregular tiny holes. It can always be identified by its lovely red wax rind, and its creamy yellow body. It's a table cheese, makes great snacks, can be well-used in cooking, and goes great with beer and wine.

EMMENTALER

This beautiful cheese is commonly known here as Swiss Cheese, and is readily identified by its large holes. It is a hard smooth cow-milk cheese, and is termed, the "original" Swiss Cheese. You will like it to make sandwiches, or for snacks, thinly sliced in salads, for dessert with fruit, and with wine and beer.

GOUDA

Another succulent bit from Holland. It is a semi-soft to hard cheese made from cow's milk and has tiny holes. Like its friend the Edam, it also sports a red wax rind, and has a creamy yellow body. It also has a nutty flavor which makes it a natural partner of fruits, wine and beer, and as a dessert cheese.

GRUYERE

This lucious cheese also has tiny holes, and comes from Switzerland. It has a flavor that corresponds with its cousin Emmentaler, and it too has a myriad of uses. Snacks, table cheese, great for cooking purposes, melts easily, and, goes well with fruits and wine.

JACK CHEESE

This cheese, which is very popular in the West is made from cow's milk. It is basically a mild, Cheddar-type cheese, and is generally semi-soft. A harder type, made from skim milk is excellent for grating. It is most often used in cooking.

LIEDERKRANZ

An American cheese, abhored by a few, loved by many. It is a soft-ripened, white-mold cow milk cheese, quite creamy in texture. The flavor to say the least is strong, and the aroma is even stronger! However, when you try it on some dark rye bread, along with a stein of dark beer, or on a light cracker, with a light well-chilled wine, you will find yourself sighing in contentment.

MUENSTER

A semi-soft smooth cow-milk cheese from Germany. It has a creamy white body with a light tan crust. Set it upon the table to nibble on between courses, or serve it as a dessert, or try it as a sandwich cheese.

PORT DU SALUT

This is the Trappist made cheese that I mentioned in the introduction. It comes from France, and is a cow-milk cheese with a firm and buttery texture. This glorious cheese wears a russet colored crust, which encloses a creamy yellow body. Try this on your guests the next time you serve some cocktails, or accompany it with a golden sherry. It also makes a fine dessert cheese, one that even Brillat-Savarin would enjoy, along with his port.

ROQUEFORT

This rare and lovely delight is another moldy cheese. It is semi-soft, sometimes crumbly and is a blue-mold sheep milk cheese. Mix it in with your next salad dressing, or dips and serve with a robust red wine.

STILTON

If you were to live in England and frequent a place called, "Simpson's," to indulge in their world famous roast beef, the chances are that after dinner you would partake of some fine old Stilton cheese. And what a treat you would be in for!

Stilton is a blue-mold cow-milk cheese that is semi soft and crumbly. It has a strong rind, enclosing a light tan body marbled with a blue-green mold. Traditionally, it is served with unsalted crackers and a glass of fine old Port. It can, however, be served as an appetizer, used in salad dressings, snacks, especially for dessert, and sometimes in cooking.

> *"Then Jacob gave Esau bread and pottage of Lentils; and he did eat and drink, and rose up and went his way" (Genesis 25:34).*

Although Esau was primarily interested in the pottage, he might well have liked the bread had it been prepared in the classic "Strata" manner, which includes generous helpings of cheese, as well as various spices, all put together to make a superb entree.

Cheese has often been referred to as a natural miracle, and as such it has sustained life for centuries. How many times have you read of the wanderer who subsisted on a bit of bread, some olives, and cheese. Cheese lends itself to countless dishes, giving them flavor as well as food values.

One interesting way it can be served is:

A CHEESE STRATA

8 slices bread
4 slices sharp Cheddar cheese
4 eggs, beaten
2 cups milk
1 tsp minced onion
2 tsp Dijon style mustard
½ tsp salt
Sweet green pepper rings

Sweet red pepper rings
Bacon strips

Carefully cut the crusts from the bread, and then cut the loaf into eight equal pieces. Place four of the pieces in the bottom of a shallow baking dish. Mix together the eggs, milk, mustard, onion, and salt and set aside for a few minutes to meld.

Now place a slice of cheese on each bread slice; then cover with the remaining bread slices. Pour the milk-egg mixture over all, and let stand a few minutes longer. Bake in a 350-F oven until the "Strata" is golden brown. Garnish with the pepper slices, and with crisp bacon slices, if desired.

> *"And thou shalt have goat's milk enough for thy food, for the food of thy household, and for the maintenance for thy maidens"*
> *(Proverbs 27:27).*

The ancients discovered the wonderful qualities of cheese made from goat's as well as cow's milk very early in time. Among other things they learned that it is an excellent substitute for meat, because it contains proteins, fats, and minerals.

A good deal of cheese was made and consumed in Bible times, and it was transported to all the lands around the Mediterranean, as well as throughout the vast Roman Empire.

Whenever and wherever people gathered, cheese was an integral part of their eating, and such is the custom today. (How about a cheeseburger?)

You might start off a festive occasion with:

A WINED CHEDDAR CHEESE

1 lb sharp cheddar cheese finely chopped or shredded
2 tbs butter
1 tbs honey
A dash Tobasco
½ cup port wine

Put in a blender, the cheese, butter and honey. Dash with the tobasco, and blend well. Now slowly add the port wine, using the blender at slow speed. Blend until it is nice and creamy. Transfer it to a crock or other covered dish and refrigerate. Serve with various crackers.

"The trees went forth on a time to anoint a king over them; and they said unto the olive tree, reign over us" (Judges 9:8).

It is reported in history that a sacred olive tree was kept in the court of the temple of Pandrosus, on the acropolis, Athens; and there is an allusion in the Psalms, (Ps 52) that indicated they were grown in the temple court on Zion.

It is a known fact that they were of tremendous importance to both the commerce and the religion of the Biblical lands, and their use as food, along with other fruits of the Lord's bounty made them almost indispensible. Here is one way to combine them with sardines to make a superb salad.

A MOUNT OLIVET SALAD

1 cup pitted ripe olives, halved
¼ cup olive oil
2 tbs lemon juice
½ tsp oregano
Salt & pepper
1 small head lettuce
¼ cup chopped green onions
2 med potatoes, cooked & sliced
3 med tomatoes cut in wedges
2 cans sardine in olive oil, cut in pieces
1 bunch radishes, sliced
1 cup crumbled Jack cheese
chopped parsley

Olives, lemons, cheese and sardines were all plentiful in Palestine, and an inventive wife might have put them together with the other condiments something like this. For a lovely decorative effect, take some of the outer lettuce leaves and line the salad bowl. Take the remaining leaves and tear them into bite-sized pieces, and pile them in the middle of the bowl.

Sprinkle the chopped green onions on top.

Next, in layers, place the tomatoes, sardines, parsley, radishes and top with the cheese. Place the halved olives here and there and make a ring of them around the heaped other ingredients.

Make a dressing of the olive oil, lemon juice, oregano, salt and pepper. Mix well, and just before serving, spoon over the salad.

(Note: this can also be garnished with a few wedges of lemon).

This recipe was quite probably accompanied by a lovely bottle of wine from the valley of the grapes in the land of Canaan!

> *"And they gave him a piece of cake of figs, and two clusters of raisins; and when he had eaten, his spirit came again to him" (I Samuel 30:12).*

It has been recorded somewhere in the annals of time, that the Egyptians were the first to note that grapes left on the vine lost moisture and that this resulted in a sweeter berry, containing more sugar. The drying of grapes to make raisins was raised to a fine art by the Bible folk, as well as by the Greeks and the Romans. During the Middle Ages, they became an important part of the trade of the Hanseatic League.

They were, of course, widely used in biblical times, because they kept well, were nourishing, and provided energy. They also combine with a number of other condiments and foods, to make any number of delicious dishes. One of which is an:

ARABIAN SALAD

3 cups, diced, cooked chicken
¼ cup puffed raisins
¼ cup puffed golden raisins
¼ cup slivered blanched almonds
ice box lettuce
1 bunch parsley, chopped
¾ cups mayonnaise
¼ cup orange juice
Freshly ground black pepper

To puff the raisins, cover them in water, bring to a boil, and let them stand for a few minutes, and then cool. After they have been cooled, add to all the other ingredients; toss well and chill. Serve on crisp leaves of well washed and crisped lettuce.

> *"But ye shall offer a sacrifice made by fire for a burnt offering unto the Lord; two young bullocks, and one ram, and seven lambs of the first year: they shall be unto you without blemish" (Numbers 28:19).*

Skewered meat is as old as time.

You can rest assured that many a Biblical shepherd placed pieces of lamb on a stick or reed of some sort which he could hold over the hot coals. This recipe can be used on your outdoor barbecue or put under the broiler in your stove. Either way, it comes out as a delicious meal. Especially when served with rice or bulghar, and a well chilled tossed green salad.

ARABIAN SKEWERED LAMB

½ small leg of lamb, (about 3 lbs) cubed
⅓ cup olive oil
1 tsp ground coriander
1 tsp ground cumin
2 whole cloves
1 one-inch stick cinnamon
1 tsp finely minced fresh ginger
½ tsp garlic, minced
½ tsp salt
¼ tsp cayenne pepper

Give this lots of "TLC" and you'll have a superb meal!

Bone the lamb and cut it in 1½ inch cubes. Pour the oil and all the remaining ingredients into a blender and blend until the spices are coarsley ground. (About 2 minutes at high speed). Pour over the lamb and marinate overnight. Fasten the meat on skewers and broil, basting occasionally with the marinade.

"A well chilled Vin Rose" might give this a bit of zest.

> *"And it shall come to pass in that day, that a man shall nourish a young cow and two sheep; and it shall come to pass, for the abundance of milk that they shall give he shall eat butter, for butter and honey shall everyone eat that is left in the land" (Isaiah 7:21-22).*

It is axiomatic that wherever there was milk and honey, there was cheese. Cheese to nibble on, to spread and to melt. Cheese has been as much a part of religion as has wine, largely because of its great nutritive values. It was made a part of every meal in many monasteries, and in the case of the Trappist monks, it has become an export of their order just as Benedictine has become an export of their order, and wine has become that of the Christian Brothers.

The Trappist cheese is called Port Salut, which is a creamy, semi-soft cheese, with a mild flavor much like that of a Gouda. However a cheese that is created nearer home that I often use is a mild Cheddar, which I incorporate into a sauce for:

"A TURKEY SALMIS"

Left over, cooked turkey, sliced
¼ cup butter
¼ cup flour
2 tbs minced onion
¼ tsp pepper
¼ tsp salt
2 dashes Worcestershire sauce
1 dash Tobasco
1 cup milk
2 cups grated mild cheddar cheese
English muffins

Place the turkey slices, both white and dark meat, in a shallow baking dish, and heat them in a slow, (250-F) oven.

Meanwhile, in a saucepan, melt the butter, and slowly stir in the flour. Add the onions and gently cook for one minute. Add the salt and pepper, Worcestershire Sauce, Tobasco, milk, and the grated cheese. Stir over a low heat until the cheese is melted and everything is well blended. Place the warm turkey slices on halves of toasted English muffins and pour over the sauce. Garnish with parsley, if desired.

> *"I have gathered thy children together, even as a hen gathereth her chickens under her wings" (Matthew 23:37).*

The partial quote from the Bible in the Gospel according to Matthew is the only reference to chicken in the Bible. However it has been pretty well determined that the domesticated bird we enjoy today originated somewhere in Southeast Asia, quite possibly as early in time as 1200 or 1300 B.C. As time has passed, this "Early Bird," has literally gone around the world to become a major source of food for every nation on earth.

Certainly the people of Israel were well acquainted with this toothsome fowl and its eggs and made good use of it in many ways; one of which might have been:

"AN ISRAEL ORANGE CHICKEN"

1 large frying chicken, cut up
Flour
Salt & pepper
¼ cup butter
¼ cup sliced sweet red pepper
1 large onion, thinly sliced
2 cups fresh orange juice
¼ cup orange honey
1 tsp fresh grated ginger
½ tsp ground nutmeg
1/8 tsp ground cloves
¼ cup each pitted black & green olives

As time neared for the men to come in from the fields, an Israeli lady would:

Very lightly coat the chicken with the flour, salt and pepper mixture and then brown the pieces in the butter in a Dutch Oven. After browning, she would remove the chicken pieces and set aside, and keep them warm. In the fat remaining in the kettle she would gently saute the onion and pepper rings until they were soft but not browned.

Then she would return the chicken to the kettle. Meanwhile she would have combined the orange juice, honey, ginger, nutmeg and the cloves. This would be poured over the chicken pieces, and the whole brought up to an easy boil. The olives would be added, the heat lowered, the kettle covered, and place in a 350-F oven and baked until the chicken was very tender.

She might even have garnished it with orange slices, along with some sprigs of fresh watercress or parsley for color.

> *"And he said unto his servant, set on the great pot and seethe pottage for the sons of the prophets" (II Kings 4:38).*

For more than 2,000 years, the Phoenicians and the Egyptians were familiar with iron, but it was not until later times that it was mined in any large quantity. The first iron they knew of were meteor fragments and were called, "Daggers from God." Actually it was the hated and feared Philistines who really developed the mining and refinement of iron, using it to make armor, implements, ornaments, and cooking pots.

And it might have been just such a large pot that was used by Elisha's servant, when she prepared his favorite pottage. In case you don't have a favorite here is a recipe that combines chicken with the Matzo meal of the Passover.

"ELIJAH'S POTTAGE"

(NOTE) The trick with this soup is to use chicken feet to give it added strength and flavor. They should be skinned which is easily done by washing them and placing them into a kettle with boiling salted water to cover. When the skins loosen, plunge them quickly into cold water and slip off the skins and discard them.

1 large chicken
2 pairs chicken feet
8 cups water
2 carrots, sliced
½ cup thinly sliced celery
2 onions, halved
1½ cups chicken broth
4 sprigs fresh parsley
1 tbs salt
½ tsp pepper
Matzo Marrow balls

Combine the chicken and the skinned chicken feet in a large pot. Cover with the water and the chicken broth, and then add all the remaining ingredients except the matzo balls. Cover and simmer over low heat for at least one hour, until the chicken is very tender. Remove the chicken and set aside, and strain the soup. Add the matzo balls, and allow to simmer fifteen minutes longer, before serving. The reserved chicken may be boned and cut up and used for other purposes.

MATZO MARROW BALLS

1 large marrow bone
2 eggs, slightly beaten

2 tbs water
1 tbs seasoned chicken stock
2 tsps grated onion
1 tbs minced parsley
½ cup matzo meal

Purchase cut pieces of marrow bone so the marrow can be easily removed. Beat the marrow together with the slightly beaten eggs and water, until the mixture thickens. Then add the other ingredients, except the matzo meal. Mix well and then stir in the matzo meal a bit at a time, until the mixture is quite thick.

Cover and place in the refrigerator to chill for about one hour. Moisten your hands with cold water and form the mixture into small balls. Let cook in the soup for about 15 minutes just before serving.

> *"And to every beast of the earth, and to every fowl of the air, and to every thing that creepeth upon the earth wherein there is life, I have given every green herb for meat: and it was so" (Genesis 1:30).*

When chicken first appeared in Europe, having been carried across Asia to Europe, it was regarded as a sacred bird. Publius Claudius, a high ranking Roman Admiral in the 3rd century B.C. desired to bring himself some good fortune so he offered his chickens food, and when they wouldn't eat, he had them hurled into the sea.

In this country, chicken was the primary dish served at Mount Vernon for General Lafayette during his visit there. I doubt there is any other fowl on the face of this earth that can be prepared in so many different ways.

A way that lends itself to an earthenware cooker is called:

CHICKEN OF THE EARTH

¼ lb lean bacon, diced
4 tbs butter
8 small white boiling onions peeled
1 leek, (white part only) thinly sliced
A 4 to 5 lb roasting chicken
1 cup dry white wine
1 tsp salt

¼ tsp pepper, fresh ground
½ tsp rosemary
½ tsp thyme
1 clove crushed garlic

Saute the bacon until crisp and browned. Remove the bacon and reserve. Melt butter and in it saute the onions, carrots, and leeks until vegetables are nice and tender. Now remove the vegetables and brown the chicken in the same frying pan. Truss the chicken and place it in an earthenware pot, and spoon the vegetables and the diced bacon all around the chicken and pour over the white wine. Season the chicken with the spices and garlic and cover and roast in a preheated oven at 400-F for 2 or more hours until chicken is tender.

"But the stranger that dwelleth with you shall be unto you as one born among you, and thou shalt love him as thyself; for ye were strangers in the land of Egypt: I am the Lord your God" (Leviticus 19:34).

The folk of all the Middle East were noted for their hospitality. The tired and weary stranger was almost always welcomed with open arms, and more often than not, the lady of the household prepared a special dish to make the stranger feel at home. This same custom traveled across the seas to our country, incidentally, where hospitality became a tradition. Especially in the South, which is as noted for its hospitality as was the Middle East. One of the many dishes often served the weary traveler is:

SOUTHERN FRIED CHICKEN

We'll pretend this came from the southern part of Israel!

2 (3 lb) frying chickens, cut into serving pieces
4 eggs
¾ cup milk
½ cup corn meal
¼ lb butter and
½ cup oil
Salt and pepper

THE GRAVY
3 tbs fat from the skillet
3 tbs flour
2 cups half and half warmed
Salt and pepper

    Melt the butter and the oil together over a medium hot heat. (Please do not use a high heat as it only burns things and dries them out!) While the mixture is heating, combine the eggs and the milk in a bowl.
    Lightly salt and pepper the chicken pieces and dip them in the egg and milk and then the corn meal and coat them well.
    Place them a few at a time in the heated oil in the skillet. I suggest you start with the dark meat pieces first, and then, after a few minutes, follow with the white meat pieces. Turn them often to make certain they are evenly browned on all sides. As they become golden brown, remove them from the skillet to an oven casserole, and when all the chicken has been browned, put on 2 cookie sheet and heat in a 350-F oven for 15 to 20 minutes.
    During this period, make the gravy.
    Measure 3 tbs of the cooking fat out of the skillet and discard the remainder, being very careful not to lose any of the brown bits clinging to the bottom. Return the bits to the pan. Stir in the flour and heat, letting the flour lightly brown. Slowly add the heated half and half and cook and stir until thickened. Season to taste with the salt and pepper.
    Present this chicken to your weary guest along with mashed potatoes, corn on the cob, hot corn bread, with lots of butter, a tossed green, crisp salad, and serve the gravy separately in a warmed gravy boat.
    For the "welcome" toast, and to drink with the dinner, I would suggest a Traminer, well chilled.

> *"To speak evil of no man, to be no brawlers, but gentle showing all meekness to all men" (Titus 3:2).*

    Throughout this epistle, you have to stress gentleness in the preparation of food. Each food has its own succulent juices and flavors and over-cooking can ruin any meat or vegetables. When the good Lord created the bounty of the earth, he endowed all manner of things with flavors, aromas, and textures, which when properly blended together can make for some remarkable gourmet dining. This method of preparation especially applies to chicken for chicken has a flavorful tenderness that is uniquely its own, but one which must never be scorched out of the bird!

Prepare your chicken with lots of "TLC," and instead of a tough, stringy mess, you will have an aromatic, sweet, tender morsel with which to please your taste buds. These pieces of chicken require a light red wine to give them piquancy.

I have named it (after a city on the Island of Cyprus) Chicken Salamis. Salamis was the first city visited by Paul and Barnabas after leaving the mainland port of Selucia.

"And when they were at Salamis, they preached the word of God in the synagogues of the Jews; and they had also John to their minister" (Acts 13:5).

CHICKEN SALAMIS

2 small (2-lbs) frying chickens
1 tsp flour
1 tbs very finely chopped onion
½ cup light red wine
¼ lb butter

Wash the chickens and dry them. Prepare them by cutting down each side of the backbone and the neck, and then lift these pieces out. Now flatten the chicken on a cutting board, skin side down and break the rib cages away from the breast bone. Pull out the breast bone.

Divide the breast from the rest of the body, and then cut off the wing. Now shear off the legs from the body, and separate them at the joint.

Make certain the chicken is thoroughly dry. Lightly salt and pepper it, and dredge it with flour, shaking off the excess.

Now gently cook the pieces of chicken in the butter, turning them from time to time, partly covered for 30 minutes. Saute until the skin is golden brown. Remove the breast pieces. (Test them by piercing them with a fork. The juice that runs out should be clear). Cook the remaining pieces for a few minutes longer, until done. Remove the chicken to a warm platter, and to the juices in the pan, add the flour onions and the wine and simmer until the sauce is slightly thickened. Return the chicken and gently simmer it in the pan for about 5 minutes.

To serve, arrange on a platter and surround with fresh vegetables in season. Pour the sauce over the chicken.

FISH

One of the great miracles performed by Jesus was that of the loaves and the fishes.

He performed many miracles of a striking nature at Capernaum, and it was there that he called Matthew to the Apostleship, as he was sitting at the receipt of customs.

Jesus' discourse on the bread of life, which followed the miracle of the loaves and fishes, and the feeding of the 5,000, and many other sermons were delivered at this ancient place on the shores of the Sea of Galilee.

> *"Then Jesus called his disciples unto him, and said, I have compassion on the multitude, because they continue with me now three days, and have nothing to eat; and I will not send them away fasting, lest they faint in the way.*
>
> *And his disciples say unto him, whence should we have so much bread in the wilderness, as to fill so great a multitude?*
>
> *And Jesus sayeth unto them, how many loaves have Ye? And they said, seven and a few little fishes.*
>
> *And he commanded the multitude to sit down on the ground.*
>
> *And he took the seven loaves and the fishes and gave thanks, and brake them, and gave to his disciples, and the disciples to the multitude.*
>
> *And they did all eat and were filled"* (Matthew 15:33-37).

Even unto this day, the Sea of Galilee, where Capernaum was located, is filled with fish of all kinds including one called St. Peter's fish. Fish that throughout time have been fried, broiled, baked, and cooked over open fires.

This cooking idea for fish may give you an incentive to feed your personal multitude with these tasty gifts from the lakes and the oceans.

A FISH CHOWDER FOR THE MULTITUDE

10 lbs fish, including heads and bones
½ cup butter
2 tbs cooking oil
1 tbs salt
2 cups chopped onion
3 large potatoes, cut into chunks

2 quarts milk
½ tsp fresh ground black pepper
½ tsp thyme
2 sprigs fresh dill

Dill weed was very common in the lands of the Israelites. And placed in combination with almost any kind of fish, it makes a very flavorful food creation.

Cover the heads and bones of the fish with water and simmer for one hour to make a fish stock.

Put the oil in a deep kettle and add the salt. Add the onions and gently brown.

Also boil the potatoes in salted water until they are just barely soft.

Strain the fish stock and add it to the kettle. Add the pieces of fish, and simmer for about 20 minutes. Then add the potatoes, the dill, and the thyme. Bring to a boil, and add the milk, and lower the heat. Let the chowder simmer for another five minutes, and add several pats of butter, and let stand for 10 or 15 minutes.

If you do this Israeli style, you will serve it with unleavened bread pieces, otherwise, use oyster crackers.

> *"Now, as he walked by the Sea of Galilee, he saw Simon and Andrew, his brother, casting a net into the sea, for they were fishers"* (Mark 1:16).

"Cyrpnus Carpio" is the ithyological name of a fish that abides in great numbers in the Sea of Galilee. It is commonly called Carp.

Originally it came from Asia, and finally came to the Middle East long centuries ago, and from thence to Europe and eventually the New World.

Legends tell of Carp living for hundreds of years, which is not true, but they often do live to be 20 and even 40 years of age, and weigh as much as 40 to 50 pounds.

Quite possibly, the lady chefs of Simon and Andrew's time used an earthenware casserole to prepare Carp brought home by the brothers.

The Sea of Galilee was sometimes called "Lake Tiberias," so we shall call this dish:

"A TIBERIAN CARP"

2 small carp (about 2 lbs each)
1 cup fine bread crumbs
Salt and pepper
1 large onion, thinly sliced
1 cup dry white wine
1 lemon sliced
pepper
2 bay leaves
Butter

Make a layer of the onion slices, lemon slices, and the bay leaves in the bottom of a casserole. Salt and pepper the Carp and coat them with the bread crumbs. Lay them on the sliced vegetables and pour in the wine. Place in a 350-F oven for 45 minutes until the fish flakes easily. Remove the fish to a warm platter, and strain the liquid in the casserole. Mix a little of the liquid with the softened butter and the flour and add it to the remaining liquid in the casserole. Simmer and stir until the sauce is slightly thickened. Correct for seasoning and pour over the fish. Garnish with parsley and serve.

"Behold, I will send for many fishers, saith the LORD, and they shall fish them" (Jeremiah 16:16).

The Mediterranean, or the Great Sea, as it was often referred to, also supplied food for the Israelites. Some of the creatures within it crawled or were without fins or scales and thus were deemed to be unclean. But there was, and still are an abundance of edible fish for the peoples on all sides of the sea.

France, Spain, Italy, the lands of the Golden Crescent, and all of North Africa reap their seafood bounty from the ocean.

One fish that is very popular is Bonito, and this way of cooking it will assuredly heighten your appetite as well as that of your friends.

BONITO FROM TYRE

1 large piece Bonito, or Albacore; head and tail removed
2 or 3 stalks celery, with leaves
5 or 6 small hot green chili peppers

1 tomato, cut in 8ths
a generous dash oregano
good pinch thyme
olive oil
salt and pepper
2 or 3 garlic cloves, peeled and halved

Wash the fish thoroughly in cold water and remove any bloody membrane. Place the garlic cloves in a cup of olive oil and let it marinate. (This can be done a day or so ahead of time, so the oil has a rich garlic flavor).

Salt and pepper the cavity of the fish, and then rub with some of the garlic olive oil.

Now stuff the cavity of the fish with a stalk or two of celery, 1 or 2 green peppers, 4 pieces of tomato, a dash of each of the spices, and then repeat the process until all the ingredients have been used up.

Sew up the cavity, using kitchen string, or skewers, and then run a spit through it, and use a bit more of the kitchen string to tie it firmly to the spit. Make certain it is as evenly balanced as possible.

Now wrap the spitted fish with two or three thicknesses of cheese cloth, and tie it with string, every two or three inches. Brush the fish well with more of the garlic olive oil, and place on your barbecue over medium coals. Baste often with the garlic olive oil. A large piece will require 2 to 2½ hours cooking time.

To serve, remove the cheese cloth, twine, and place on a platter garnished with sliced tomatoes and greens.

> *"And Simon, answering said unto him, Master, we have toiled all the night, and have taken nothing, nevertheless at thy word I will let down the net.*
> *And when they had this done, they enclosed a great multitude of fishes; and their net broke"* (Luke 5:5-6).

The encyclopedia records some 35 kinds of fish in the Sea of Galilee, one of the most prominent being fresh water bass. There are a number of varieties of bass, all of them interestingly enough, named after colors; white, black, silver, yellow, and calico.

The fishing done in Simon's time was done in small open boats with nets as well as with fishing poles and hooks. Simon, Peter, and Andrew all made their living by fishing, and all lived in Galilee. Capernaum, where Jesus preached, was essentially a fishing town, and it was from there that he set out on his fateful journey to Jerusalem, accompanied by Simon, Peter, Andrew, James and John, all fishers from the Sea of Galilee.

A STUFFED BAKED BASS

If you can get your fisherman to catch a 3 or 4 pound bass.

1 bass
3 eggs
1 tbs water
1 tbs each chopped parsley and chopped green onion
Salt and pepper
1 cup dry white wine
½ cup half & half
1 cup finely crumbled french bread crumbs
2 egg yolks
some lemon slices

If it hasn't already been done for you, clean the fish. Then mix together the bread crumbs, parsley, salt and pepper, and the green onions. Stuff the fish with this mixture and close the cavity.

Place in a large baking dish and pour the wine over.

Bake in a pre-heated 400-F oven for about 30 minutes. Be sure to often baste the fish with its pan juices. Remove the fish from the dish and keep warm. Pour off the pan juices and strain into a sauce pan and boil until reduced by half. With a fork, whip the egg yolks and the half and half together, and then add to the pan juices.

Return to the fire and cook over low heat until the sauce is thickened. Place on a bed of fresh watercress and parsley sprigs, and surround with lemon wedges.

> *"And they gave him a piece of a broiled fish, and of a honeycomb.*
> *And he took it, and did eat before them"* (Luke 24:42-43).

The Sea of Galilee has borne many names down through the years. "The Sea of Chinnereth," "The Lake of Gennesaret," "Lake Tiberias," and in this day and age it is known as, "Bahr Tibariya."

Somehow I like "The Sea of Galilee" best, because as a young lad I was enchanted with the Bible stories of Jesus walking on the water, with his instructions to the fishermen to cast their nets, and how their catch very nearly swamped their boats, and how he recruited some of his most staunch disciples from among the fishers of Galilee.

Fish were, of course, an integral part of the diet of people of those times, just as they are in our time.

One way the folk around Galilee and Capernaum might have prepared a prize catch was to grill it.

A FESTIVAL FISH

Several fish steaks, cut about 1 to 1½ inches thick
Salt and pepper

THE BASTING SAUCE
½ cup white wine
½ cup olive oil
2 tbs lemon juice
2 tbs grated lemon peel
¼ tsp oregano

Place the fish steaks on the grill with a drip pan underneath. Brush them well with the basting sauce, and grill them over medium coals. Baste them from time to time, and turn them once.

Test the fish steaks with a fork, and when they flake easily, they are done to a turn! Give them lots of attention, and do not let them overcook or they will become dry and tasteless.

> "The Earth is the Lord's, and the fullness thereof; the world, and they that dwell therein. For He hath founded it upon the Seas, and established it upon the floods" (Psalms 24:1-2).

A fish that fulfills all the requirements of the Bible admonitions with respect to the creatures of the seas is the Sea Bass; a fish common to most of the oceans of the world and especially the Mediterranean.

There are recorded accounts of Bass in Egyptian lore and they were a substantial part of the Israeli living on the sea coast of the Promised Land.

And they are still today an important item of the diet of all the lands surrounding the Great Sea.

SEA BASS A LA CANAAN

1 whole medium-sized Sea Bass
2 quarts (or enough to cover) Court Bouillon
Hollandaise Sauce
Chopped parsley
24 whole small white potatoes
dill weed
butter

Make a Court Bouillon for fish, which has been slightly salted. Place the fish in it and when it has come to a boil, lower the heat and let simmer gently and poach until it is done.

Place it on a heated dish, and garnish with the parsley. Serve with the Hollandaise sauce and the small potatoes cooked with dill weed.

"Simon Peter went up, and drew the net to land full of great fishes, an hundred and fifty and three; and for all there were so many, yet was not the net broken" (John 21:11).

Pickled or preserved fish has been a favorite of those folk who originated in the Holy Land, and it is indeed a favorite the world over. There are many kinds of fish that can be pickled in many ways, according to the land where they are netted. A great favorite of mine is pickled herring, and although this way of doing it does not come from a land near the Sea of Galilee, it does come from a country that loves God just as much as those in Palestine.

SWEDISH GLASSBLOWERS HERRING

2 salted herring, cleaned, scraped and soaked in cold water for 12 hours
A 1½ inch piece of fresh horse radish root, peeled and thinly sliced
1 carrot, peeled and sliced
1 large red sweet onion, peeled and sliced
½ piece ginger root, peeled and sliced
2 tbs allspice
2 tsps whole mustard seed
2 or 3 bay leaves

THE LIQUID FOR PICKLING:
¾ cup white vinegar
½ cup water
½ cup sugar

Wash and clean the herring and bone them thoroughly. Be sure to get out all the very thin tiny bones.

Cut the herring into 1-inch pieces.

Now prepare the pickling liquid. Mix together the vinegar, water and sugar, and bring to a boil in an enamel saucepan, and then bring to a boil. Remove from the heat and let cool. Place a layer of onion slices in the bottom of a glass jar, (1-quart size), top with a few slices of herring, add some carrot slices, ginger root and horseradish.

Scatter a bit of the allspice, mustard seed and a bay leaf. Keep repeating the process until the jar is full. Pour the pickling liquid into the jar, cover tightly and let stand in the refrigerator for two or three days. This makes a wonderful appetizer, and if you don't dole it out carefully, you'll find it will quickly disappear.

"Therefore, thou shalt speak unto them this word; Thus saith the LORD God of Israel. Every bottle shall be filled with wine" (Jeremiah 13:12).

Certain archeologists assert that wine originated some 10,000 years ago. The Bible indicates that when Noah's Ark finally settled on Mount Ararat, and the flood water receded, one of the first projects Noah accomplished was to plant a vineyard.

Wine was not used or regarded as an intoxicant by our ancestors; rather as something to be honored and used to clear one's palate and to flavor foods.

WINED HALIBUT STEAKS

4 Halibut steaks
1 cup Chablis wine
Salt & pepper
1 cup Matzo meal
½ cup butter
2 tbs butter

1 onion, chopped
½ sweet red pepper, chopped
½ sweet green pepper, chopped
1 tsp curry powder
Lemon juice

Let the fish steaks marinate in the wine for about 15 minutes. Then salt and pepper them, and dredge them with the matzo meal. In a large heavy skillet, melt the butter and gently brown the fish steaks. Place them in a casserole.

In a saucepan, melt the additional butter, add the chopped onion, and the chopped peppers, and gently saute until the vegetables are soft. Add the curry powder and mix well.

Continue to cook for a few more minutes, stirring. Add the wine from the marinade along with the lemon juice and bring to a boil, constantly stirring. Lower the heat and simmer for one minutes.

Pour the sauce over the fish steaks in the casserole, and cook in a 450-F oven for about 10 minutes, until fish is tender and flakes easily.

Transfer the fish steaks carefully to a serving platter, and pour the sauce left in the casserole overall.

> *"That lie upon beds of ivory, and stretch themselves upon their couches, and eat the lambs out of the flock, and the calves out of the midst of the stall" (Amos 6:4).*

Sound a bit like a decadent Rome? You can wager it does! But you must admit they at least had the good taste to appreciate Lamb. All the Romans enjoyed lamb's succulent meat, and ate it roasted, broiled, baked, and stewed or braised. One way a noble Roman Patrician might have enjoyed a fine leg of lamb could be called:

A CENTURION'S LAMB

2 or 3 tbs olive oil
1 (5 to 6 lb) leg of lamb
2 tsps salt
¾ tsp pepper
1 tsp rosemary
2 cloves garlic

2 tbs flour
½ cup hot water
½ cup white wine
3 anchovy fillets, minced
2 tsps flour
2 tbs water

While resting between wars, Caesar may have had his chefs prepare his leg of lamb this way.

Heat the oil in a large dutch oven or roasting pan. Add the leg of lamb and brown well on both sides.

Mix 1½ tsps salt, the pepper, rosemary and garlic, (which has been crushed in a bit of the salt) and the 2 tbs flour. Rub this all over the surface of the lamb, using the back of a wooden spoon. Add the hot water, wine, and anchovies to the pot, cover and roast in a 325-F oven for about 2½ hours, until the meat is tender.

Remove the lamb to a serving platter and keep warm. Strain the pan drippings to remove the spices.

Mix the flour and water to make a smooth paste, and stir into the drippings. Cook and stir until the sauce thickens. Stir in the remaining salt.

Serve with the sliced lamb along with a nicely chilled Rose, and love the Lord for his blessings!

"And God made the beast of the earth, after his kind, and cattle after their kind" (Genesis 1:25).

Research tells us that the cooks of the Exodus built the open fires against a wall of stones, wherever possible, as the back wall acted as a chimney of sorts, and also provided an additional heating surface.

You can duplicate this by taking some fairly heavy wire mesh and making a 3-sided slim box about 6 inches wide at the top and 4 inches wide at the bottom, and 12 to 15 inches high, open at the top. Place this at the back of your home barbecue, fill it with charcoal, and you have the perfect means for spit roasting. Doing this will enable you to place a drip pan under the meat, to catch any fat as well to catch your basting liquid, which can then be used over and over to keep the meat moist and tender as it cooks.

A ROAST OF GALILEE

1 whole beef fillet

FOR THE MARINADE:
a large onion, chopped
1 clove garlic, finely chopped
¾ cup red wine vinegar
¼ cup water
¼ tsp ground cloves
¼ tsp ground cinnamon
1 tsp seasoned salt
6 crushed peppercorns
½ cup red wine

In a large bowl combine the onion and garlic and mix well. In a saucepan combine the vinegar, water, cloves, cinnamon, seasoned salt, and the peppercorns. Bring to a boil; remove from the fire and let cool. Now add the red wine, and the chopped onion and garlic. Mix well and pour over the roast, which has been placed in a large shallow baking pan or dish. Let it marinate at room temperature for at least 4 to 5 hours. Turn it from time to time to make certain it absorbs the marinade flavors on all sides. When ready, place it firmly on a spit and tie it with kitchen string at 2-inch intervals. Make certain it is evenly balanced.

Place a drip pan under the roast and let cook for 30 to 40 minutes, dependent upon the degree of doneness. Baste frequently with the marinade.

When it is done, remove the strings and place the roast on a serving platter, decorated with fresh watercress, and let the head of the household slice it at the table.

Be sure to use a very very sharp knife!

Pour a fine California Burgundy with this, or a chilled "Rose," if you prefer.

> *"And they brought their cattle uno Joseph: and Joseph gave them bread in exchange for horses, and for the flocks, and for the cattle of the herds" (Genesis 47:17).*

There are nearly 150 mentions of cattle in the Bible ranging from Genesis to the Prophets to the New Testament. As mentioned earlier in this book,

Moses made the keeping of their herds a stipulation for the release of the Children of Israel from Egypt. During the forty years of privation in the Wilderness, cattle and their breeding were of prime consideration. They provided milk, cheese, leather, and food just as they do today. This respect for beef extended over the known world of Biblical times from the lands of Ghengis Khan to Darius of Persia, and throughout Africa.

There are 22 basic cuts of beef, all of which lend themselves readily to the creation of tasteful dishes. And not all of them have to be expensive cuts. Here is an interesting recipe using sirloin tips and fruit.

BEEF FROM THE FERTILE CRESCENT

½ cup dried apricots
½ cup dried figs
1½ tbs butter
1½ tbs olive oil
2 tsps seasoning salt
½ cup chopped onion
1 tbs chopped parsley
2 cups beef stock
2½ lbs cubed sirloin tips
½ tsp fresh grated ginger
1 clove garlic, chopped
¼ tsp fresh ground black pepper
1 stick cinnamon
6 whole cloves
1½ cups hearty red wine

Cut the fruit into eighths and place them in a saucepan with enough water to cover and bring to a boil and then simmer for about 15 minutes, until they have soaked up most of the water.

In a large kettle, heat the butter along with the oil, and then gently brown the pieces of beef. Sprinkle them with seasoned salt as they are browning. Now add the onions, and cook them only until they start to turn color. Add the beef stock, the spices, cloves and the wine. Mix thoroughly and cover and simmer for 1½ hours until the meat is tender. Take out the cinnamon stick and serve with noodles.

"And the man increased exceedingly, and had much cattle and maid servants, and men servants and camels and asses" (Genesis 30:43).

The ancestry and the exact time of the domestication of cattle has not yet been ascertained, however it has been established from fossil discoveries that they were probably native to parts of Europe, Africa, and Asia, which certainly brings them into the purview of the Holy Land's inhabitants.

It has been surmised that man hunted cattle in early times, much as we hunt deer today, but very soon domestication became of prime importance in order to insure a regular supply of meat. This need was undoubtedly behind Moses' demand that the Pharaoh release the herds along with the Hebrew peoples.

Cattle were often considered sacred, as they are still today by some religious castes in India. And aside from their use as food, they have been used as a power supply. Perhaps the old time carts should have been rated in cattle power!

Since Moses was such a superb general, he designated authority to other leaders and some of them quite possibly enjoyed:

A HERDER'S STEAK

1 (2 to 2½ inch) thick porterhouse steak
Salt and freshly ground black pepper
Garlic olive oil
Red wine vinegar
Lemon juice
lemon quarters
chopped parsley
Black olives
Parsley sprigs

Sprinkle the steak with the salt and pound the ground pepper in on both sides with the palm of your hand. Mix together in a shallow flat dish, the garlic olive oil, wine vinegar, and then add the steak and let it marinate for at least one hour, turning occasionally.

When ready, place on a barbecue grill over nicely greyed coals, and cook for about 8 to 10 minutes on each side, depending upon the rareness you desire.

Place on a serving block, sprinkle with the lemon juice and parsley, and garnish with the lemon quarters, olives, and parsley sprigs.

"For every beast of the forest is mine, and the cattle upon a thousand hills" (Psalms 50:10).

If you are an admirer of the great American cowboy, and his tall tales of the great cattle drives, and of riding the range, you'll appreciate this recipe for a genuine prairie stew.

I'm not at all certain how the chuckwagon chefs of Christ's Time prepared it, but in the early days of Americana, our chuck wagon cook put all the elements together, and hung it on the back of his wagon enclosed in a large container full of charcoal and the embers from the campfire of the night before and as the herds moved on throughout the day, the stew automatically stirred and cooked itself, and was ready for the evening meal, when camping time came.

"A RANGE RIDER'S STEW"

1½ lbs stew meat, cut in 1-inch cubes
2 tbs all-purpose flour
1 tsp salt
2 tbs shortening, or cooking oil
1½ cups very strong coffee
2 tbs molasses
1 clove garlic, minced
1 tsp salt
1 tsp Worcestershire sauce
½ tsp oregano, crushed
1 good dash Tobasco sauce
1½ cups water
4 carrots, cut in 1 inch slices
10 small white cooking onions
8 or 10 small new potatoes
¼ cup cold water
3 tbs flour
1 cup, (or more) burgandy wine
1 tbs pepper
1 large can stewed tomatoes

First: The day before, in the evening, place the beef cubes in a bowl along with enough red burgandy wine to cover; cover the bowl and let the meat marinate overnight in the refrigerator.

The next day, remove the cubes from the wine and reserve the wine for later use. Mix the flour and the salt and pepper and coat the beef pieces well.

In a large Dutch oven, brown the cubes gently until they are brown on all sides, using the shortening or cooking oil.

Now stir in the coffee, molasses, garlic, a bit more salt, the Worcestershire, oregano and give the whole thing a dash of tobasco sauce. Add about ½ cup of the reserved wine, cover and simmer for about 1½ hours. Now add the 1½ cups water, the carrot chunks, onions, and potatoes. Taste the cooking liquid for seasoning, and if you like it a bit more flavorful, add a touch more of the reserved wine.

Simmer the stew for another 30 minutes, until the vegetables are tender. Mix the flour in with the cold water, and add to the stew. The stew liquid should be relatively thick. Cook and stir until this is achieved. Be careful to stir to prevent burning. Add the canned tomatoes and cook for another 15 minutes. Stir well and serve.

The fig is one of the favorite foods in the Near East, and its export plays a large and effective role in its economy. The productiveness of the fig tree was often considered a token of peace, and of Divine favor.

"And he spake to them a parable; behold the fig tree, and all the trees.
When they now shoot forth, ye see and know of your own selves that summer is now nigh at hand" (Luke 21:29-30).

The fruit of this lovely tree, combined with other fruits of the soil such as walnuts, oranges and butter and flour work together to make a bread of delightful flavor and one that I know you will enjoy.

ORANGE FIG BREAD

½ cup butter
¼ cup honey
½ cup light brown sugar, packed
1 egg, beaten
1 tbs grated orange peel
½ tsp vanilla
½ cup buttermilk
2½ cups sifted all-purpose flour
2 tsps baking powder
¼ tsp baking soda

½ tsp salt
½ cup orange juice
1 cup chopped dried figs
1 cup chopped walnuts

Cream together the butter, honey, and sugar until fluffy. Add the eggs, orange peel and the vanilla and beat again until light and fluffly. Stir in the buttermilk.

Sift together the flour, baking powder, baking soda, and salt.

Add to the cream mixture alternately with orange juice, mixing after each addition. Stir in figs and nuts. Turn batter into a 9x5 inch loaf pan and bake at 350-F for 60 to 70 minutes. Cool slightly and turn out onto a cake rack for more cooling before slicing.

"I will abundantly bless her provision: I will satisfy her poor with bread" (Psalm 132:15).

When David, in his psalms to the Chief Musician, sang of bread, he expressed the love and respect in which it was held by all people, rich and poor alike.

It was often used in religious ceremonies and still today, is eaten in celebration of the Sabbath, as well as other holy days.

Here again, as with most foods, there can be slight variations, but research has shown that the basic "Challah" bread has remained the same down through the years.

This recipe comes from Israel:

CHALLAH (AN EGG BREAD)

½ cup warm water
1 pkg active or 1 cake dry yeast
½ cup milk (warmed)
½ lb sweet butter
2 tbs sugar
4 beaten eggs
4 cups flour
1 tsp salt
2 tbs salad oil
1 egg yolk

1/8 tsp saffron
Poppy seed

Dissolve the yeast in the warm water. Melt the butter and add the warm milk and sugar until the sugar is thoroughly dissolved. Now add the yeast mixture. Mix in the beaten eggs, and transfer the mixture to a large bowl. In another bowl, sift together the flour and salt. Make a hollow in the center of the flour mixture and pour in the egg-yeast mixture. Mix together to thoroughly blend the ingredients.

Add more flour if needed. Now exercise your muscles and fingers and blend until you have a smooth, elastic dough, adding more flour as needed.

Shape into a nice round ball and place in a well greased bowl, cover and place in a warm draft-free place to rise until it has doubled itself. (Brush with the oil on top.)

Take the dough out and return it to your floured surface and punch it down, and knead it a bit more.

Set it aside and let it rest for about 15 minutes.

Divine the dough into 8 pieces. And on your lightly floured surface, shape each piece into a rope a little less than 2 feet long. Make a standard braid using three of the ropes, and place them on a well buttered baking pan. Braid 3 more ropes and repeat the process. Put a few inches of distance between the first braid and the second (about 1½ inches).

Braid the remaining ropes and place them on top of the other two over the center.

Brush with the beaten egg yolk and sprinkle with lots of the poppy seed. Cover again and let rise for another hour and then bake in a 375-F oven for about one hour.

Happy holiday!

"Then Abigail made haste, and took two hundred loaves, and two bottles of wine, and five sheep ready dressed, and five measures of parched corn, and an hundred clusters of raisins, and two hundred cases of figs, and laid them on asses" (I Samuel 25:18).

A great favorite of people of all ages is raisin bread. And when I say ages, I mean youngsters, middle age folk, and oldsters as well as the centuries of time past.

Combine raisins with some milk, yeast and flour, plus a few other ingredients, and you will have a bread fit for the angels.

ANGELIC RAISIN BREAD

2 cups milk
1 pkg active yeast
2 oz butter
2 eggs
4 oz honey
1/8 tsp salt
½ lb seedless, golden raisins
8 cups flour

The basics of this fine recipe were born in the kitchens of a great hostelry in the West many years ago.

I'm sure, however, that its forebearer was a version used in the Holy Land. Warm the milk and dissolve the yeast in it. Then add the butter, the eggs, the honey, salt and the raisins. Thoroughly mix. Then stir in the eight cups of flour, a little at a time, until you have a smooth dough. Keep mixing as you go, because this can get quite stiff. Place the dough in a well buttered bowl, turn it to coat all of it, cover and let rise in a draft-free place for three hours.

Punch the dough down, and fold it, and then divide it and put it in well buttered bread loaf pans, and cover and let rise again for about 1 hour.

Bake in a 350-F oven for 45 to 50 minutes, until the tops are golden brown.

"And Gideon went in and made ready a kid, and unleavened cakes of an epah of flour" (Judges 6:19).

As I wrote in the beginning of another recipe, unleavened breads cover a wide area of the Eastern world.

One nation, which is not Biblical, but which excels in the baking of unleavened breads is India, where such bread is often the basic food of life.

These folk use it in many ways, one of which is to stuff it; sometimes with meat, and sometimes with vegetables. Used and prepared in Palestine, such a stuffing might include lentils.

"A LENTIL STUFFED BREAD"

2 cups all-purpose flour
2 cups whole wheat flour
1 tsp salt

3 tbs melted butter, or margarine
water

FOR THE FILLING:
1 cup dried lentils, soaked in water overnite
oil for frying
½ tsp aniseed
½ tsp salt
1 tsp curry powder (or more to suit your taste)
2 tsp chopped parsley

Make the unleavened bread. Mix together the flour and salt, and add enough water to make a SOFT dough. Knead quite well then cover and set aside in a floured and buttered bowl for one hour in a draft free place.

Return it to a lightly floured surface and knead it again and then roll out quite thin, and cut it into 2-inch circles. In the meantime, drain the lentils, and crush them coarsely in a blender or with a morter and pestle.

Heat the oil, and gently saute the anise seed. Then add the crushed lentils, salt, curry powder, and some well crushed red pepper, if desired. Stir and fry for 5 minutes. Add the chopped parsley and let cool.

When cool enough to handle, place a small teaspoon of filling on one side of the bread disc. Place another disc on top and seal the edges by brushing them with milk, and pressing them together.

Very gently roll them out a bit to flatten them slightly, and then fry them in quite hot deep fat, until both sides are brown.

(These will also make fine hors d'oeuvres).

> *"And in every province, and in every city, whithersoever the King's commandment and his decree came, the Jews had joy and gladness, a feast and a good day"* (Esther 8:17).

No feast, large or small, whether in Bible times, Roman times, or in our time would be complete without a fine dessert. Any magnificent dinner, with all its flavors and sauces must have something to ease the palate, and sweeten the taste. Such a function is served by a dessert, whether it be a pie, or a cake, or a custard, or a fruit.

To those of Bible areas, dessert was more often than not a handful of dates, or some pomegranates. Later in the Roman Empire, people became more fanciful. Water ices were developed and eventually made their way from the Bible lands, across Europe to end up in America as ice cream and sherbets. Combinations of ice creams make for colorful and exciting desserts.

Tortes, cakes, tarts, pies all have a common ancestry, and all can be served with almost any meal. Fruits are especially useful for uncloying the jaded appetite.

Whatever you serve with your feast, bear in mind that you are presenting a combination of the Lord's gifts to your guests, and to make yours and their evening more blessed.

This dessert is not exactly an ointment meant for soothing aches and pains, but it will certainly sooth your stomach after a grand and sumptuous dinner.

It is a grand way of preparing a pound cake. Pound cakes originated way back in time and the original recipe called for a pound of sugar, a pound of butter, a pound of flour, and so on.

Today's recipe is about the same, except, for a spice or two, and some other condiments that have been added.

AN ORANGE POUND CAKE

2 cups butter
2¼ cups sugar
8 eggs
5 cups sifted cake flour
½ tsp salt
½ cup grated orange peel
½ cup ground almonds

THE FILLING:
1 cup orange marmalade
2 cups whipping cream, whipped
2 tsps instant coffee
6 tbs powdered sugar
1 tsp vanilla
⅔ cups toasted, slivered almonds

Soothe your palate by creaming the butter, and adding the sugar until it is light and fluffy. Now add the eggs, one at a time, beating well after each addition. Sift all together the flour and salt. Slowly add to the butter mixture, along with the almonds and the orange peel.

Blend thoroughly. Pour into two well greased loaf pans, and bake in a preheated oven at 275-F for 2½ hours. Remove and cool on a rack.

Now slice the two cakes into 5 layers each. Spread all but the top layers with the filling marmalade. Reassemble with the plain slice on top.

Now mix together the coffee, sugar, vanilla, and add to the whipped cream. Frost the top and sides of the cakes, and sprinkle with chopped almonds and candied orange peel, if desired.

> *"Therefore the Jews of the villages, that dwelt in the unwalled towns, made the fourteenth day of the month, Adar, a day of gladness and feasting, and a good day, and of sending portions one to another" (Esther 9:19).*

Sending portions, one to another, probably originated our long time custom of sending jams, jellies, and fruit cakes, one to another on our feast days.

Most of these portions were rich, sweet, and fruity in composition. And some of them down through the years have become modern day desserts. One of them is a variation of Crepes Suzette, which, interestingly enough originated in the land of the Pharaohs.

A MEMPHIS DESSERT

⅔ cup flour
1 tbs sugar
Salt
2 eggs
2 egg yolks
1¾ cups milk
2 tbs melted butter
2 tbs orange flower water

FILLING:
1 (10-oz) jar orange marmelade
½ cup chopped almonds
1 pint, heavy cream, whipped
orange blossoms, or candied orange peel

Now, while barging down the Nile, sift altogether the flour, sugar and salt. Add the two whole eggs and the egg yolks and mix until smooth. Add the milk, melted butter and the orange water, and mix again. Let stand in the refrigerator for two hours before using.

When ready to use, stir and thin with a bit of water if the batter is too thick. Heat a small heavy skillet, and coat it very lightly with oil. Pour in one very thin layer of the batter; just enough to coat the bottom of the pan, and then turn the pan round and about to evenly spread the batter.

Cook until the edges barely start to brown and then flip over and cook the reverse side. Stack the crepes as they are finished and store them in the refrigerator until they are to be used.

Just before serving, spread each crepe with the marmelade, leaving a small unfilled margin around each edge. Sprinkle with the almonds and place a large dollop of whipped cream in the center. Roll up the crepes and serve garnished with the orange blossoms or the candied orange peel.

"Behold he smote the rock, that the waters rushed out, and the streams overflowed" (Psalms 78:20).

Water. The clear cold sparkling without which there would be no life. Neither flora nor fauna nor mankind can survive without it. And, of course, it is an integral part of most all food preparation, as it has been from time immemorial.

One of the earliest desserts recorded in use by the nations of the Golden Scimitar, were water ices. And they are enjoyed as much today as they were long ago.

They are light, easy to digest, and can be made in just about any flavor you may choose. After a good lunch or dinner, try this:

A REFRESHING WATER ICE

1 pint fruity white wine
juice of 2 lemons
juice of one orange
1 cup sugar
2 cups water
1 cup whipped cream
lemon curls

Prepare the syrup by mixing the sugar and water, and bringing to a boil for three minutes, and then let cool. Then add the wine, lemon juice, and the orange juice. Mix well and put in the freezer compartment until it is quite solid. When ready to serve, gently fold in the whipped cream and serve in sherbet glasses, and garnish with the lemon curls. Serve immediately.

Chapter Seven

Three Great Gourmet Dinners

"The destiny of nations depends on how they nourish themselves." Jean Anthelme Brillat-Savarin (1755-1826)

The foods, both animal and vegetable, as well as the fruits of the sea, and those of the land, coupled with a myriad of spices and herbs have made life for all mankind potentially a paradise on earth.

And for some, these wonderful gifts of the Lord our God, have created a veritable Garden of Eden. Those who have ventured into this land of milk and honey, and of plenty, are today known as Gourmets.

Their numbers are many. Certainly Solomon was one of the first. Preceding him were certain Pharaohs of Egypt, who enjoyed both animals and fowls, as well as various grains, beer, and wine.

Undoubtedly there were others about the world, who, as time passed took their pleasure from glorious repasts. Ghengis Khan and his love of a rare Shishkabab. Eric the Red and his penchant for the fish off the coast of Iceland. Henry the 8th, who dearly loved a hearty roasted Royal Hart from Scotland.

And in later times, men such as Brilliat-Savarin whose uses of spices revolutionized the world of gastronomy. And who once traveled for days aboard ship, crossing all the way from France to America just to sample an American turkey and to try a Philadelphia turtle soup. Also, Carame, the first of the great chefs of modern times, followed by Escoffier and Louis Diat, who created "Vichyssoise." I will include, in this chapter, an original recipe for this incredible potage. Try it on a warm summer's eve, with a proper wine, and truly live for a moment in the "Garden of Eden."

I once was associated with a great gourmet, who, twice a year, traveled from Los Angeles to New Orleans to dine at Antoine's.

Ture Wretman, a friend and great restaurateur, prepares a "Kalv Fillet Oscar" that is unparalleled. Only you have to go to Stockholm to enjoy it. And while you are there go to a small restaurant called, "Konsnars Huset."

If your mood is more to the meaty side, there is a restaurant across from what used to be the stockyards in Chicago, that will serve you a Kansas City corn-fed steak 2-inches thick, along with eggs, and steaming baskets of sliced broiled potatoes, and parsley.

Diamond Jim Brady was, of course, noted for the enormous cuts of prime roast beef that he consumed. He was a great Gourmet and a Gourmand!

To be a true Gourmet, one must take into account the texture of the food, the taste, the aroma, as well as the compatibility of the sauces, the service, and manner of presentation. Not to mention the ultimate pleasure it gives your palate.

The Gourmet dinners that follow are not altogether Biblical, but they are all inclusive of the gifts of the LORD, and as such they are to be genuinely enjoyed!

DINNER NO. 1

"And God said, let us make man in our image, after our likeness: and let them have dominion over the fish of the sea" (Genesis 1:26).

In my humble opinion one of the great blessings that the good LORD gave us that flourishes in the waters, is the provider of the most elegant of all palate pleasers: Caviar.

And interestingly enough, the finest in the world, Beluga, comes from a Biblical land of yore, now known as Iran.

It is possible that the folk of Bible times did not know of this rare delicacy, but since it came from a fish bearing fins and scales, I'm sure they would have considered it clean, and worthy of gustatory attention.

There are a few rules regarding Caviar, which must be observed in order that you and your guests may enjoy it to the fullest.

Firstly, not only the Caviar but the serving dish must be very, very cold.

I can remember attending a Red Army Day celebration at the Russian Legation in Stockholm, Sweden in 1945, and walking into a large room, featuring an enormous crystal bowl, embedded in a 100 pound block of ice, reposing upon the table. With it to one side, were platters of lightly toasted black and rye bread, and bowls of sweet butter. There were also Persian limes, and quartered lemons.

Now you do not have to serve ice cold Vodka with this, but if you serve Caviar to start your Gourmet dinner, you will most assuredly start it off with elegance.

If at all possible, use glass or crystal dishes and serving spoons, as any metal will destroy the delicate flavor of the roe. Silver may look very lovely, but your gourmet guests will disdain it.

If you don't want to serve it plain with toasted breads, an interesting way to serve Caviar is with "Blini," a light pancake, made as follows:

BLINI

1 cake yeast
2½ cups warm milk
2 cups sifted flour
2½ cups buckwheat flour
2 eggs
4 tbs butter
¼ tsp salt
½ tsp sugar

Soften the yeast in the warm milk, and then stir in the flour and stir until the mixture is smooth.

Cover and let stand in a draft free place for eight hours. Then uncover and add the buckwheat flour and mix well. Separate the eggs, and beat the yolks with the softened butter, and add to the flour mixture. Add the salt and sugar, and cover and let stand for 3 more hours.

Lastly add the beaten egg whites, let the batter rest for another 15 minutes, and then pour the batter off the top without stirring. The batter should be the consistency of cream. Cook them in melted butter until they are done. Serve them heaped with Caviar and whipped sour cream.

All gourmet foods require attention and care during their preparation. This culminates in extracting the essences that take these foods above that of the ordinary table. Such a food is a fine, clear, rich consumme. Its aroma will whet anyone's appetite and its taste will hone it.

A most elegant titled gentleman, with whom I once shared such a consumme was Major General Count Folke Bernadotte of Wisborg. The son of a prince of the royal house of Sweden, Count Bernadotte devoted his life to the service of others. He was head of the Boy Scouts, on the boards of numerous charities, and, in the end gave his life for people all over the world. He was the first ambassador of the United Nations and was assassinated in Crete where he was attempting to establish peace between the new Israel and the Arabs.

One of his favorite places to dine was the Opera Kjelleren, which was across the street from the Foreign Office, located in the cellar of the opera house. A speciality of the restaurant was consumme julienne, and if you have the time and patience, here's a relatively simple way to put it all together.

CONSUMME JULIENNE

(This is actually composed of two soups, and it will take some time to prepare. However most of it can be prepared in advance and refrigerated).

FOR THE BOUILLON:
3 to 4 lbs beef bones, and 2 lbs veal bones
1 large carrot, sliced
1 large onion, sliced
5 quarts water
2 cups water
Beef or veal trimmings
Chicken carcasses, (from leftover roasted chickens)
1 tbs salt
6 peppercorns
4 or 5 celery stalks, including tops and leafs
4 to 5 sprigs parsley
1 large tomato
2 leeks, chopped
1 onion, chopped
1 carrot chopped
1 clove garlic, chopped

Ask your butcher to cut up the beef and veal bones into medium sized pieces. Spread them in a shallow roasting pan and spread over them, the sliced carrots and onions. Roast the bones in a 400-F oven until they are well browned. Remove them to a large soup kettle, and add 5 quarts water. Bring to a boil.

Add the 2 cups water to the fat remaining in the roasting pan, and over direct heat, bring it to a boil, scraping up all the bits of browned meat clinging to the pan. Add this liquid to the soup kettle along with any beef and veal trimmings. (If you don't have any, ask your butcher for some). And if you have any left over chicken carcasses, either from fried or roasted chickens add them as well. Now add the salt, peppercorns, and bring everything slowly to a boil. Skim off any scum as it rises to the surface. Add the celery, parsley, tomato, leeks, onion and carrot, and the garlic. Remove the last of the scum, cover and cook simmering, for 4 to 5 hours.

Don't stir during this period of cooking! Let cool sligtly and ladle out as much of the clear liquid as you can. Add another cup of cold water to the kettle, and let it settle. Ladle out the rest of the clear liquid, and strain it through several thicknesses of cheesecloth.

FOR THE CONSUMME
3 quarts of the bouillon
1½ lbs coarsley chopped lean beef from the neck or the forequarter
1 carrot, chopped
2 leeks, chopped
2 stalks celery, chopped
2 cleaned and skinned chicken feet
2 egg whites
carrots, green beans, leeks, celery or turnips cut in thin strips
Butter

Thoroughly chill the bouillon and remove all the fat. Place in a large kettle, and add the coarsely chopped beef, a carrot, the 2 leeks, and the 2 chicken feet, as well as the 2 egg whites, slightly beaten. Bring it slowly toward a boil, but stop stirring before a boil is reached. Cover and simmer for one hour.

Let it cool enough to handle, skim off any scum, and strain through at least 4 thicknesses of cheese cloth. Ladle into another very clean kettle and set aside.

In the meantime, cut the carrots, green beans or any of the other vegetables you have chosen into thin strips, and add them to 1 or 2 tbs butter and 2 or 3 tbs of the consumme, in a small saucepan. Cover the pan with a piece of well buttered wax paper with a hole cut in the center, and braise them gently for 20 minutes. Drain and add to the consumme just before serving.

> *"As birds flying, so will the Lord of Hosts defend Jerusalem; defending also, he will deliver it; and passing over, he will preserve it" (Isaiah 31:5).*

The incredible man I'm about to introduce certainly was in a way a defender and a deliverer. His flying involved the ancient city of London during World War II.

Czechoslovakian born Vladamer Tobyishka was one of those described so well by Sir Winston Churchill as the "FEW" that so bravely fought the Battle of Britain.

Banned from his beloved homeland by the Nazis, "Toby" fled to the forces of freedom, and became a leader in the air war against oppression. Glider pilot, fighter pilot, and bomber pilot, and a deeply religious man who believed fervently in peace.

I first met him at Snetterton Heath, an American B-17 airbase in mid-England, where he came as a visitor from the R.A.F. Bomber Command.

We became good friends and quickly found we shared a mutual love of fine food. And so, from time to time, when we could match our leaves, we "hied" away to the Highlands to angle for those lovely succulent Scottish trout; a fresh water fish, that in my opinion has no peer.

Freshly caught, cleaned, and either pan fried or baked, along with a salad, a dessert, and perhaps a wee drop or two of the Ambrosia of the heather, and you will have the cockles of your heart warmed indeed!

For your elegant dinner, here is your second course.

TROUT TOBYISHKA

6 (¾ lb) trout, cleaned and split.
12 slices bacon
1 tsp salt
½ tsp fresh ground black pepper
4 tbs chopped parsley
parsley sprigs, that have been dampened and crisped

Line a large baking dish with the slices of bacon. Wash and dry the trout well with paper towels, and lay them skin side down on the bacon. Sprinkle them with the salt and pepper and with the chopped parsley. Cover the dish with foil, sealing it around the edges as tightly as possible.

Bake for 25 to 30 minutes at 350-F and then test to see if the fish flakes easily with a fork.

When done, place the trout on individual serving plates; top each one with a single slice of bacon, and surround with a sprig or two of fresh parsley.

Chop the remaining bacon and sprinkle each of the trout, lightly. Serve garnished with thin lemon slices.

> *"He shall feed his flock like a shepherd: He shall gather the Lambs with his arm, and carry them in his bosom, and shall gently lead those that are with young" (Isaiah 40:11).*

Such a man was Reitmeister Baron Sager, who as the Swedish Consul-General to New York in 1907, the Charge D'Affaires of the legation in Riga, Latvia after the Russian revolution, and finally as the Camp Liaison Officer for the American Internee camp at Loka Brun in Sweden, gave much of his life to tending the flocks of people, he was asked to care for.

I first met Baron Sager in 1944, when I was assigned the care and feeding of over 1800 American Air Force men interned in Sweden.

A stalwart and very noble man, the Baron maintained a summer home near the camp, where he entertained in a most lavish manner. "Margarita Holm" was situated on over 7,000 acres, which were kept by a huge army of Share Farmers, field workers, and various other kinds of help.

As was his wont, when I first arrived at the camp to inspect it, he gave a dinner in my honor.

Visualize, if you will, a great dining hall, crystal chandeliers, thick white linen napery, candles, heavy highbacked chairs, sideboards loaded with silver trays, and on a long table, exquisite settings of fine bone china.

Behind each chair stood a footman in full livery, including white wigs, white silk stockings, short black satin pantaloons, and red waistcoats emblazoned with the Baron's crest.

The "Piece de Resistance?" Barons of Lamb borne to the waiting guests at the table on a huge silver tray, carried by four footmen!

It may be not in your interest to go quite that far in serving your guests, but you can pleasure their palates with a lovely:

BARON OF LAMB

A Baron of lamb, including both legs
lard
water
small new potatoes
dill weed
salt and pepper
parsley
watercress

Rub the baron with salt and lightly with pepper. Lay a few thin slices of lard across the top of the baron, and as it cooks, baste it from time to time with the drippings in the pan.

Place the baron in a large roasting pan, and roast in a 400-F oven for ½ hour, basting frequently. Then reduce the heat to about 375-F and continue to roast for another three hours. Baste often and watch the color so it does not become too brown. It must come out of the oven super elegante.

About ½ hour before the end of the roasting time, add the peeled potatoes, sprinkled with a little dill. Make certain there is still enough liquid in the pan so they will cook and gently brown.

Transfer the baron to a large serving platter, and surround it with mounds of green beans, bright green peas, and cherry tomatoes, interspersed with the potatoes, and garnished with sprigs of watercress. Carve it at the table.

(Note: This is a rather large serving. Should you desire you can roast a leg along with a part of the loin, or the rack and shoulder may be cooked together. Or you can simply do a nice lovely large leg of lamb).

"A friend loveth at all times" (Proverbs 17:17).

"Start Tape" "Speed" "Slate it" "Corris Guy" Show number 51, taped April 6, 1964 for playback April 10, 1964.
Director: Bob Robb
"Okay, fade up on camera one; cue music, and matte title slide; take the matte out, and cue Corris."
That was the opening scenario for a grand culinary television show that was produced by and starred in by a good friend, who did indeed give of her talents, love, and affection, Ms. Corris Guy. A true epicure, an authority non-pareil on food, and food consultant to Lawry's Foods and restaurants.

Baskin-Robbins, and the National Turkey Growers Association, just to mention a few.

Corris cooked on television in Los Angeles for more than 15 years, and I was privileged to direct many of her shows. The dishes were varied; all chosen to help people learn to properly cook and thusly to eat better. Among her many talents was the fine art, (and it is an art!) of creative salad making, and I believe this particular epicurean salad will enhance your Baronial meal.

(Note: This dinner has been planned in the Continental manner, therefore the salad will follow the Entree, not precede it. Its use is to freshen the palate).

A COLORFUL ENDIVE SALAD

12 belgian endives
4 or 5 cooked beets
salt
chives, chervil, and tarragon, finely chopped

Carefully clean the fresh endives and chill them slightly. Place 2 endives on small salad plates, and sprinkle each plate with chilled cooked beets that have been sliced in very thin julienne strips.

Moisten with a bit of vinaigrette sauce, (French Dressing made with wine vinegar and a wee touch of garlic). Sprinkle over each plate a mixture of the chives, chervil, and the tarragon.

DINNER NO. 2

"Build ye houses, and dwell in them; and plant gardens, and eat the fruit of them" (Jeremiah 29:5).

A world famous house that thousands of people from all over the world have dwelt in and there enjoyed the fruits of a multitude of gardens is the St. Francis Hotel in the "Bagdad of the West," San Francisco. And it is there that this particular appetite inspiring first course was developed by the Chef de cuisine, Mr. Victor Hirtzler.

Celery was first found in Asia and was certainly available to the people of Bible lands. Its first use was as a medicine, but later in the 15th or 16th century it was cultivated as a food by the Romans. There are many versions of this dish, however, one I like, and one I think Chef Hirtzler would approve is a:

BRAISED CELERY

6 celery hearts
chicken stock
4 carrots, sliced
2 medium onions, sliced
Salt and pepper
1 tbs kitchen Bouquet
2 or 3 sprigs parsley
Anchovies
Pimiento strips
Hard cooked eggs, sliced

DRESSING:
1 part teragon vinegar
3 parts olive oil
1 pinch ground tarragon
Salt and fresh ground black pepper

Thoroughly clean the celery hearts and remove any tough outer stalks. Split them into two or three pieces, lengthwise, depending on their size.

Place them in a shallow pan on top of the sliced carrots and onion, and pour over them the chicken stock. Use just enough to barely cover the celery. Sprinkle them with the chopped parsley, and salt to taste. Cover with foil and simmer over a low fire for five to ten minutes until the celery is tender. Remove the celery from the dish and chill.

Serve two pieces to each guest, topped with alternate strips of pimiento, and anchovies, interspersed with slices of the hard cooked egg.

Sprinkle more chopped fresh parsley on top.

> *"And the child grew and was weaned: and Abraham made a great feast the same day that Isaac was weaned" (Genesis 21:8).*

Great feasts have been a means of celebrating events since the beginning of time. The ancient Egyptians, Israelis, Romans and Greeks all used a feast to mark an occasion of joy and happiness.

And since, I'm sure, your occasion for a gourmet dinner such as this is one of happiness and pleasure, I shall recommend as a second course, a grand potage that was created by one of the most joyous and talented Chefs of all time, Monsieur Louis Diat, Chef D' Cuisine of the world famous Ritz Hotels. Ranked among the great chefs of the world, along with Carame, and Escoffier, Monsieur Diat took an everyday soup from his childhood in Vichy, France, and elevated it to the esteem of princes and kings.

VICHYSOISSE

4 leeks
1 onion, sliced
2 tbs butter
5 potatoes, peeled and sliced
1 quart chicken broth
1 tbs salt
2 cups milk
2 cups cream
chopped chives

Carefully wash and clean the white parts only of the leeks. The best way is to cut them lengthwise in half and then wash them to make certain all the gritty material is washed away.

Place them in a large saucepan along with the onions, in the butter, and saute them until they are just barely gold in color. Be very careful that they do not brown! Add the sliced potatoes, the chicken broth and 1 tbs salt. Boil gently for 35 to 40 minutes. Now place the mixture in a blender, and puree, and then return it to the saucepan and the fire. Add the milk and cream, and season to taste. Bring to a boil; remove from the fire, and let cool to room temperature and then rub the mixture through a fine sieve. When it becomes cold enough, add one more cup of cream and then chill very well. Serve sprinkled with chopped chives.

> *"And it shall come to pass, that the fishers shall stand upon it from En-gedi even unto En-eglaim; They shall be a place to spread forth nets; their fish shall be according to their kinds, as the fish of the great sea, exceeding many" (Ezekiel 47:10).*

There is not much room left in the hustle and bustle of these days for the courtly gentleman and the gracious lady of more courteous times gone by.

One such gentleman, however, who adheres to those delightful customs and with whom I have been privileged to have a relationship is the very fine actor, Mr. Gene Raymond, a believer in the Lord, and his works, especially those contained in Acts, Chapter 20, Verse 35.

> *"I have shewed you all things, how that so labouring, ye ought to support the weak, and to remember the words of the Lord Jesus, how he said, it is more blessed to give than to receive."*

Although fortune has been kind to Gene Raymond, he has passed much of it on to help those less privileged; especially those afflicted with Arthritis. For more than a decade, he has devoted much of his time, talent, and money to the search for a cure.

I first met him a number of years ago, when I had the pleasure of directing him and his lovely lady, Jeanette McDonald, in the presentation of the Rose Parade on ABC.

Both Gene and Jeanette graced the silver screen; he as the urbane gentleman, and she as a fine singer-actress, often the co-star of Mr. Nelson Eddy.

Recently, when producing a fund-raising show for the Las Floristas Headdress Ball, which benefits several crippled children's clinics, I again encountered Gene, as usual, lending his charm and presence to a worthy cause.

A widely traveled and very knowledgeable gentleman, he has become a recognized gourmet over the years. His penchant, being that of a person with the grand manner, is, of course, the Classic French Cuisine.

"A FILET OF SOLE"

½ cup dry white wine
½ bay leaf
6 whole black peppercorns
½ tsp salt
a sprig of fresh dill (or parsley)
1 clove garlic, halved
2 lbs filet of sole (or more if needed)
Lemon juice
White wine sauce
Chopped parsley

1. In a large saucepan, combine the white wine, bay leaf, peppers, salt, dill, garlic and ½ cup water. Bring to a boil, and simmer slowly uncovered, for about 15 minutes. Remove from the fire and set aside.

2. Preheat your oven to 350-F. Now wipe the sole fillets dry with paper towels, and sprinkle them with lemon juice. Then fold each fillet into thirds, (the dark side inside), and arrange them in a shallow baking dish.

3. Strain the mixture over the fillets of sole, and cover the dish tightly with foil. Cook the fish in the oven for 15 minutes. Then remove them from the oven and the dish and drain them carefully. Strain the liquid left in the baking dish and reserve one cup for the white wine sauce. Meanwhile, keep the fillets warm on a heated serving platter. Make the white wine sauce and pour over the fillets, and sprinkle each serving with some freshly chopped parsley.

WHITE WINE SAUCE

¼ lb. fresh mushrooms
2 tbs butter
2 tbs flour
½ tsp salt
1 cup strained cooking liquid from the sole
¼ cup dry white wine
½ cup heavy cream
1 egg yolk, slightly beaten

1. Wash the mushrooms and slice down through the stem.
2. Melt the butter and add the mushrooms and saute for about 5 minutes. Then add the flour and the salt and stir until smooth.
3. Very gradually stir in the cooking liquid from the fish, and add the wine and the cream.
4. Bring just to boiling, constantly stirring. Reduce the heat and simmer very gently for five minutes.
5. Stir a little of the hot mixture into the egg yolk, and mix well. Return it to the saucepan and mix again. Simmer gently, a few minutes longer. (This will make almost 2 cups)

> "But the angel said unto him, fear not, Zacharias: for thy prayer is heard; and thy wife, Elizabeth shall bear thee a son, and thou shalt call his name, John" (Luke 1:13).

"John." In Biblical times, John the Baptist, and the apostle John. In other times and countries, King John of England, and other names; Johaan, Ian, and the french Jean, all meaning "John." I once had an uncle named John who traveled the Klondike, and fought in the Boxer Rebellion. But the most interesting "John," I ever knew was a master of television.

This tale and recipe is a gastronomic toast to as rare a chap as has ever graced the face of this planet.

John Gaunt, the youngest fellow ever commissioned in the U.S. Navy in World War II. The NBC executive that established the first NBC-TV station in Washington, D.C., and the producer-director of the original Red Skelton TV show. And finally the vice-president of radio and TV for the world-wide operations of the Grant Advertising agency.

A princely man, given to immaculate attire, conservative in appearance, but given a chance, fully capable of bursting into song, accompanied by a few well executed dance steps.

A perfectionist on stage as well as in the TV control room, and at the same time a compassionate man who would be the first to congratulate the crew for a job well done.

John was an epicure and very proud that he was a direct descendent of John of Gaunt of the War of the Roses. With this heritage, it is easy to understand his love of English foods; a favorite being—

A TRULY RARE ENGLISH ROAST BEEF

1 3 or 4 bone rib-roast
6 or 8 medium sized potatoes, peeled
Yorkshire pudding
Salt and pepper

"THE GAUNT METHOD":
Arguments have raged across land, sea, and through the air over the proper way to prepare a fine roast of beef. Some encase it in rock salt, others rub it with flour, and others sear it in a very hot oven, in order to secure browness. The following method appears to be the simplest, and one that should provide a fine and succulent dish.

Firstly, let the roast stand for at least an hour before roasting at room temperature. Cold meat never gives a true temperature reading and often arrives at the table, either overdone or underdone. And a fine roast of beef should be cooked "a-point," as the French would say.

When the roast has fully reached room temperature, place it in a large roasting pan so it rests upon the bones. Prior to this, cover it with thin pieces of fat that have been pounded thin and then tied on with kitchen string. Using an even temperature method, roast the meat at 325-F for 18 to 20 minutes per pound, if a rare roast is desired; for 23 to 25 minutes for a medium roast, and for 30 to 35 minutes per pound for well done.

The last half hour surround the roast with the peeled potatoes, and turn them once or twice so they will evenly brown.

Serve the slices of meat with the potatoes, sprinkled with a bit of freshly chopped parsley and with:

YORKSHIRE PUDDING

4 eggs
2 cups all-purpose flour
2 cups half & half
½ tsp salt
½ cup beef drippings

Thoroughly beat the eggs and the half and half. Sift the flour with the salt and gradually add to the milk-egg mixture. Beat until all is well blended, and smooth. Pour the beef drippings into a shallow baking pan, and add the batter, mixing well. Bake at 450-F for about 10 minutes, then reduce the heat to 350-F and bake another 12 to 15 minutes, until it is golden brown. Cut into squares and serve with the roast.

> *"And Ahab spake unto Naboth, saying, give me thy vineyard, that I may have it for a garden of herbs, because it is near unto my house" (I Kings 21:2).*

This introduction to our gourmet dinner salad, involves a lovely lady, whose expertise in the world of food has led her from Lawry's fine foods to my kitchen. In short, she is my wife, and I hesitate not to state that she has been a beacon in my search for culinary success.

One of the most glamorous and finest gourmet restaurants in the world is Ernie's of San Francisco. And it was at this renown waterhole that Lois proved her "Mettle D' Cuisine."

We were in San Francisco on a television assignment for the then Governor of California, the Honorable Edmund G. "Pat" Brown, and decided to take a break and dine at Ernie's. The dinner involved several superb dishes; among them a Caesar Salad. As is their custom, the dish was prepared at the table, and after watching the salad chef's tossing and mixing, Lois tasted the salad, and quite audibly said, "This is not a Caesar Salad!"

Now, I'm quite willing to admit that salads are not my forte, and, quite frankly, it tasted fine to me. And I was somewhat surprised when Lois called the Maitre D' to the table, and charmingly inquired, "May I show you how to do this salad, properly?"

The salad cart was produced forthwith, and with great gusto and much finesse, my lady proceeded to instruct the Chef D' Salade and his assistants in the fine art of making a:

CAESAR SALAD

1 large clove garlic (Marinate crushed, in 3 tbs olive oil for 24 hours)
2 tbs Worcestershire Sauce
2 tbs lemon juice
1 coddled (1-min) egg
Fresh ground black pepper
6 tbs grated Parmesan cheese
Romaine lettuce
9 tbs french dressing, (6 tbs olive oil, 3 tbs wine vinegar, 1 tsp seasoned salt and ground pepper)
Garlic croutons
2 anchovy fillets

Here's how she did it:

NOTE: In the case of a dinner such as this, relatively small portions are recommended.

Combine the french dressing, the garlic oil, cheese, and Worcestershire sauce. Let stand for several hours or overnite. In a bowl, mash the anchovie filets in a small amount of lemon juice, gradually adding it all. Grind in the pepper to taste, and add the dressing, cheese mixture. In a small separate bowl, beat the coddle egg and add to the dressing bowl. Sprinkle the courtons and extra grated cheese over torn bite sized lettuce, and pour over the dressing. Toss well, and serve immediately.

> *"Pleasant words are as a honeycomb; sweet to the soul, and health to the bones"* (Proverbs 16:24).

Such a phrase might well apply to a luscious dessert, for nothing else can bring a proper conclusion to a well-prepared beautifully served dinner.

Personally, I believe the ideal dessert for a gourmet dinner should be rich, refreshing, and rewarding to the palate as well as to one's eye.

In this case, the old expression, "From soup to nuts," to identify a complete dinner might well be paraphrased to read, "From soup to—"

A GLAMOROUS ICE CREAM ROLL

4 eggs
¾ cup sugar
½ cup sifted cake flour
¼ tsp salt
½ tsp baking powder
1 tsp ground cinnamon
¼ tsp baking soda
3 tbs cold water
4-oz chocolate squares, melted
1 pint chocolate ice cream in a square carton
1 pint vanilla ice cream in a square carton
Chocolate bits
Khalua
fresh strawberries

> *"And she took flour, and kneaded it, and made cakes in his sight, and did bake the cakes"* (II Samuel 13:10).

Make a dessert cake roll by combining the eggs with the sugar and beating until thick. Sift together the flour, salt, baking powder, cinnamon, and add to the egg mixture and mix well.

In another bowl, add the chocolate, 2 additional tbs sugar, the baking soda, and the water and mix well. Add this mixture to the egg mixture and work into a batter.

Butter a rectangular baking pan and line it with a well-buttered piece of parchment paper. (wax paper may also be used). The paper should be sufficiently large enough to cover the sides as well as the bottom of the pan. Pour in the batter and bake in 375-F oven for 15 minutes. Very carefully turn out the cake onto a kitchen towel, and remove the paper, and then using the towel, roll up the cake lengthwise, jellyroll fashion, and let cool.

Cut the ice cream square into sticks about ½ inch squares, lengthwise and freeze.

When ready, unroll the cake and place on it the alternate sticks of the ice cream, so that when it is rolled again the center will appear as a checkerboard. Roll up the cake with its filling, and pour over it additional melted chocolate until it is well coated. Sprinkle with chocolate bits or shavings and freeze.

Serve sliced with each slice lightly sprinkled with the Khalua liquor, and garnish with fresh strawberries.

GOURMET DINNER NO. 3

God did not confine himself to the Near East, by any manner of means, when he was busy creating the Earth and all the things on it. He gave generously to all of the Earth; land and sea alike. Fish, game of all sorts, vegetables, and fruits were all bounty given to mankind to thrive upon and enjoy.

And I think you will find this rather elegant dinner, which is not confined to the biblical lands most tasteful, and if you have the time and the patience, a wonderful repast to prepare for your very special friends.

> *"I am come into my garden, my sister, my spouse: I have gathered my myrrh with my spice; I have eaten my honeycomb with my honey; I have drunk my wine with my milk: Eat O Friends; drink, yea, drink abundantly O Beloved" (Song of Solomon 5:1).*

> *"I went down into the garden of nuts, to see the fruits of the valley, and to see whether the vine flourished, and the pomegranates budded" (Song of Solomon 6:11).*

As indicated earlier in this volume, cheese has played an important role in the feasting of all the folk of the Mediterranean area. And combined with nuts and some spices it has become a most flavorful and zesty appetizer.

One relatively simple way to make a combination that will please all your guests is:

A GINGER CHEESE

1 (8-oz) jar candied ginger in syrup
3 (8-oz) pkgs cream cheese
1 tbs ginger syrup
2 dashes Tobasco Sauce
finely chopped almonds, pecans, or cashews
finely chopped Maraschino cherries, both red and green

Remove the ginger from the jar and finely chop. With an electric mixer, beat the softened cream cheese until it is smooth and creamy. Blend in the ginger, the ginger syrup and a pinch of salt, and the Tobasco. Shape the cheese mixture into a nicely rounded ball, and then roll it into a mixture of the nuts and cherries.

Wrap the covered ball in foil and place in your refrigerator for several hours. When it is served, the dish may be garnished with some pieces of fruit, such as pears, apricots, and peaches.

Serve with sesame crackers.

"Awake O North Winds, and come thou South; blow upon my garden, that the spices thereof may flow out" (Song of Solomon 4:16).

Among the more exotic gifts of the Lord is the mushroom, which along with its rare country cousin, the Truffle, ranks as one of the more succulent epicurean treats. Personally, I find a small, rather thick, filet Mignon, prepared a "pointe" and then garnished with flavorful button mushrooms, can turn even a disastrous day into one of pleasantness.

Blessed with a bit of spice from Solomon's garden, a touch of oil from his olive trees, some vinegar made from the fruit of his vineyard, the mushroom becomes a most heavenly viand, as you will discover when you prepare an appetizer made of:

MUSHROOMS ANGELIC

2 (8-oz) jars of button mushrooms
garlic
vinegrette dressin
crisp lettuce

carrot curls
minced parsley

THE DRESSING:
½ tsp salt
¼ tsp dry mustard
¼ tsp garlic powder
2 tbs white wine vinegar
6 tbs olive oil
chopped capers, parsley, shallots, chervil
1 finely chopped hard-cooked egg

Pour out the liquid from the mushroom jars and discard. Leave the mushrooms in the jars and add a sliver of garlic, (peeled) or two to each jar. Make the vinegrette dressing, mix well and then pour over the mushrooms in the jars. Chill for several hours, shaking them from time to time to make certain the mushrooms are well coated.

Make a bed of crisp lettuce leaves, pile the mushrooms on top and garnish with carrot curls, celery curls, radish rosettes. Sprinkle the whole with chopped parsley, and the chopped hard cooked egg.

Serve with colored toothpicks for dainty fingers!

> *"For Lo, the winter is past, the rain is over and gone; the flowers appear on the earth; the time of the singing of birds is come, and the voice of the turtle is heard in our land" (Song of Solomon 2:11-12).*

The heritage of any great land lies much in its food, for that most necessary adjunct to the business of living has involved the wars, trade, and livelihood of all of the inhabitants since the advent of the first settlers.

As mentioned before in this book, the time of Solomon involved spices, wheat was a staple to the people of the Exodus, and grapes, cattle, and even deer nourished the residents of the Land of Milk and Honey.

A simple Hors D'oeuvre that embraces the fruit of the chicken, and some spices is:

"AN OASIS STUFFED EGG"

12 hard-cooked eggs, chilled
¼ cup softened cream cheese

¼ cup sour cream
4 or 5 tbs white wine vinegar
¼ cup chicken stock
¼ tsp garlic powder
¼ tsp white pepper
1 tsp celery salt
1 tbs curry powder
2 dashes Tobasco sauce

With a very wet and very sharp knife, carefully cut the eggs in halves, lengthwise. Remove the yolks and mash. Add to them, the cream cheese, sour cream, chicken stock, garlic powder, and the dashes of Tobasco Sauce. Mix thoroughly and with a teaspoon, carefully stuff the egg halves, rounding off the tops.

If desired, each egg may be decorated with a slice of a pimiento stuffed olive, or with a cross made of finely sliced green pepper. Serve on a platter lined with chilled, crisp lettuce leaves, and garnish with watercress.

"A fountain of Gardens, a well of living waters, and streams from Lebanon" (Song of Solomon 4:15).

A very old method of encasing foods to make them more attractive as well as enhance their flavor is to wrap them in a leafy green vegetable. In the countries about the great Sea, grape leaves are often used, as they impart flavor as well as color. Probably, the best known today are "Dolmas" which the Eastern Mediterranean countries use both as a main course and as an appetizer.

These little morsels, however, could well have originated in the Valley of Eschol, which, you will recall abounded in beautiful grape vines. Pleasured with added bits of succulent, seasoned chicken, they may well have been served to the ruler of Lebanon, when Solomon negotiated for the famed Cedars of Lebanon, which he wanted for his temple.

"A ROYAL HORS D'OEUVRE"

2 whole chicken breasts
2 cups chicken broth
Salt & pepper
½ tsp curry powder

1 jar marinated grape leaves, drained
A Lebanese dip

Salt and pepper the chicken breasts, and set them in the chicken broth, along with the curry powder. Bring to a boil and simmer until the chicken is fork tender. Remove and let cool. Then skin them and take out the bones, and cut the meat into 1-inch square pieces.

Drain the grape leaves and trim off the stems, and then thoroughly rinse. Place them in a large sieve and pour boiling water over them to soften, and then let them drain and cool.

When well cooled, cut them lengthwise in halves; place a piece of chicken at the stem end, and fold over the sides. Then roll them up completely encasing the chicken, and secure with a toothpick. Chill for several hours, and serve with a Lebanese dip.

LEBANESE DIP

¼ cup sour cream
¼ cup cream cheese
1 tsp toasted sesame seed
¼ tsp ground ginger
1 tsp Worcestershire
2 dashes Tobsco
1 tbs olive oil

Mix all ingredients together thoroughly and let refrigerate until just before serving time.

The first course of a fine dinner should be served in small quantities so as to tease the palate, and yet pleasurable enough to give the guest a hint of the superb dishes to come.

Such a light soup is:

SHERRIED CONSUMME

5 cups chicken broth
1 cup Sherry Wine
2 tbs minced green onions
¼ tsp white pepper

Combine the chicken broth, sherry wine, minced green onions, and the pepper in a saucepan and heat, stirring occasionally. This soup can be served either hot or chilled.

The "Soul" of the matter. Epicures the world over will swear by the virtues of Dover Sole, a fine flatfish found only in the waters of the English channel. And rightfully so, because it has a texture and flavor that cannot be equalled. However, in the interests of economy, and especially with the addition of the proper sauce, I have had great success with American or "Lemon" sole, as it is sometimes called. And the sauce that makes it sing, uses a fine California white wine. All together it is called:

FILLETS OF SOLE IN WHITE WINE

½ cup dry white wine
½ bay leaf
6 whole black peppercorns
½ tsp salt
a sprig of fresh dill, or parsley
1 clove garlic, split
2 pounds Fillet of Sole
Lemon juice
White wine sauce
Chopped parsley

For the wine, I would recommend a California Reisling, or a Rhine, or a Pinot Blanc. Okay? Are you ready?

In a 2 quart saucepan, combine the wine, bay leaf, black peppers, salt, dill, garlic, and ½ cup of water. Bring to a boil, reduce heat and simmer uncovered for 15 minutes. Set aside.

Preheat your oven to 350-F. Wipe fillets of sole with damp paper towels, and sprinkle them with lemon juice. Fold each fillet into thirds, (the dark side inside) and arrange them in a single layer in a shallow baking dish. Strain the wine mixture over the fillets, and cover the dish tightly with foil. Poach fish in the oven for about fifteen minutes. Then remove them and set aside in a warm place to keep warm, and strain and reserve 1 cup of the liquid for the white wine sauce.

Make white wine sauce; pour over fillets and sprinkle with chopped parsley.

WHITE WINE SAUCE

¼ lb mushrooms
2 tbs butter or margarine
2 tbs flour
½ tsp salt
1 cup strained cooking liquid from the sole
¼ cup dry white wine
½ cup heavy cream
1 egg yolk, slightly beaten

Wash mushrooms and slice thickly down through the stems. Melt butter or margarine in a medium saucepan. Add the mushrooms and saute for five minutes. Remove from the heat. Stir in flour and salt to make a smooth mixture.

Gradually stir in the cooking liquid from the fish; add the wine and the cream. Bring just to boiling, constantly stirring with a wooden spoon. Reduce heat and simmer for five minutes. Stir a little of the hot mixture in the egg yolk, mixing well. Pour egg yolk mixture back into the saucepan and mix all well. Cook, stirring for 2 or 3 minutes longer.

When you have placed the cooked fillets on a warm serving platter, gracefully arranged, pour this delectable sauce over them and garnish with the parsley, and prepare yourself for the bows you will be asked to take!

Note: In several of these recipes, I have indicated the use of heavy cream. Use an all-purpose cream, or whipping cream if the former is not available. The sauce should be very smooth and have a slightly thick consistency. And if you made it carefully, it will also have a vibrant, but subtle taste.

KALV FILET OSCAR

"All right Mr. Robb, would you please turn a bit more to the right, and this time, drop your voice level a bit, and put more feeling into it!"

That was my introduction to an adventure in good eating, as well as an enduring friendship that exists to this day. And whenever I serve "Kalv Filet Oscar," at "The Sanctuary" I save a moment to myself when I can stand alone in the kitchen and drink a silent toast in memory of a great lady, a fine actress, and a great chef and restaurateur.

I received a phone call one day from Mr. George Larson, who at the time was the Chief of Public Relations for the American Legation in Stockholm, and who was a close and dear friend; he told me that there was a gentleman from Hollywood in town who wanted to make a screen test of some kind, and since he knew that I had been involved in the theater, that maybe I could help solve his problem. His credentials were excellent, and George asked me to aid and abet, if I could. So, a luncheon meeting was arranged at Teatern Grillen across from the Royal Dramatic Theater (owned by my good friend Tura Wretman at the time), and there I met for the first time Eddie Blum.

Writer, connoisseur of good food and wine, fantastic gin player, and sometimes producer-director, Eddie Blum had conceived and written "Gilda," the great film that starred Glenn Ford and Rita Hayworth. And, in the course of events, he came up with the idea of doing a film on the American Internees in Sweden during World War II, to star James Cagney. The basic idea was that Cagney, as an American Internee, would of course meet and fall in love with a beautiful Swedish Girl, and . . . well, you know the rest. On the basis of this idea, Columbia pictures sent Eddie and his wife to Sweden to research the story. The only trouble was that both the first and second drafts of the script that Eddie sent back to Columbia didn't please the "powers that be," and Eddie was summarily fired. However, since Eddie was in Sweden, and now on his own, he decided to see if he could find another Ingrid Bergman and take her back to America with him—so the trip shouldn't be a total loss! And that's where I came in.

With all the brass of a major studio executive, Eddie walked into the revered temple of the dramatic arts in Stockholm, the Royal Dramatic Theater, and announced that he was looking for a new talent to return to America with him, and, believe it or not, they actually conducted auditions for him!

As it happens, the Royal Dramatic theatre conducts annual acting contests throughout the provinces and a certain number of the actors and actresses are given student contracts for training at the theater; the idea being that in four or five years of very hard work, they just might merit the effort. Well Eddie interviewed all the young talent and among them was a dark brunette with a very special quality, and he chose her for his great moment of discovery. Her name was Marta Toren. Remember?

Now, with equal aplomb Eddie sashayed over to Svensk Film, which was comparable to MGM in those days in Sweden, and talked them into giving him a free screen test of Marta to take back to the states with him. Of course, no one knew that his relations with Columbia had been severed. Not yet.

So Eddie took a piece of his Cagney script, and went looking for some ham to play the Cagney part so he could make the test. And that's where "yours truly" came into the picture. (That's a pun).

Well, we made the test, and believe it or not Ingmar Bergman was on the set. What he did I don't recall, but I know he was there because the senior Art Director of Svensk Film told me so. I believed him because every time he came to my flat for dinner, he always ate his wine glass at the end of dinner . . . which, as you can imagine, caused no end of discussion.

Which brings us to Kalv Filet Oscar, and Tore Wretman, and Teatern Grillen and Opera Kallaren. Sounds like a devious route, doesn't it?

At that point in time (as we say when testifying before Congressional Committees) Tura Wretman owned the famed Restaurant Riche, of which the theater grill was a part. As you can imagine, most of the theater folk congregated there and Marta, Eddie and I dined there often.

During the course of many great repasts, Tura joined us and the subject of the enjoyment of fine food naturally came up. One evening Tura suggested that I try Kalv Filet Oscar, named for a Swedish king of yore, which had been created at Opera Kallaren (which, losely translated, means the Opera Cellar). As a matter of fact it is located in the cellar of the Opera House in Stockholm and if you are a reader of the Time-Life cookbook on Swedish food you'll see some superb pictures of Swedish food laid out there. Anyhow, I'm sure that King Oscar went to his grave filled with fond memories of those nights when he regally dined in the Opera Kallaren on Kalv Filet Oscar . . .

Now, you don't have to serve this in the cellar, but if you feel in the manner Royale . . . try this on for size.

"KALV FILET OSCAR"

1½ lbs veal cutlets
¼ cup butter
½ tsp salt
1/8 tsp pepper
3 tbs chicken broth
Salt & pepper
1 to 1½ lbs asparagus, cooked
1½ curps Bernaise Sauce
Bread crumbs & milk

Cut veal into serving pieces and pound gently until 1/8 inch thick. Dip in milk, salt and pepper, and then into bread crumbs. Melt the butter in a large skillet, and then gently saute the cutlets until they are golden brown, turning frequently. Remove to a hot platter; wrap in foil and put in a slow oven to keep warm. Add chicken broth to the skillet juices and cook rapidly until the sauce is reduced by half. Add remaining 2 tbs butter to the skillet.

Arrange the asparagus spears over the veal pieces, and pour some of the pan sauce over. Top each portion with a generous dollop of the Bearnaise sauce. This dish should have a lovely light brown, red, yellow, and green color when served.

In the continental manner, some form of salad is always served following the Entree in order to cleanse the palate prior to the dessert. I personally am a great fan of fresh fruit, and therefore I most heartily recommend the following as a means of refreshing your taste buds for the dessert to follow!

CHILLED DESSERT MELON CUPS

Enough cantelopes to serve ½ cup per person, well chilled. Any fresh fruit in season: berries, bananas, peaches, strawberries, pears, small pieces of watermelon, papaya, mangoes, etc. Lemon juice.
Fresh mint leaves
Powdered sugar
Sabra Liqueur

Slice and dice the fruit fairly large. Make melon balls from other cantelopes, and place all into a large bowl. Sprinkle with the lemon juice, add the fresh minced mint leaves, and mix very carefully. Refrigerate. Just before serving, cut the melons in half, remove the seeds and pulp and discard. Heap each half with some of the fruit mixture; sprinkle with the powdered sugar, and a bit of the Kirsch, and sprinkle with some chopped mint leaves. (Whole mint leaves may be used as a garnish, if they are wet and then dipped in powdered sugar).

GLAZED TANGERINE AMBROSIA

6 tangerines, peeled, segmented & seeded
¾ cup sugar
⅓ cup water
½ cup chopped nuts
½ cup flaked coconut
Sherry wine (optional)

Place tangerine segs in a sieve over a large bowl. Set aside. In a small saucepan, combine sugar, and water. Bring to a boil over high heat, stirring until sugar dissolves. Cook rapidly for 2 minutes. Pour hot syrup over tangerines 2 or 3 times, allowing syrup to drain thru sieve, until all segments are well coated.

Allow to drain a moment, or two after final glazing. Combine tangerine segments with chopped nuts and coconut. Toss lightly to mix.

Sprinkle with a small amount of sherry just before serving.

(Makes 6 servings)